THE RELEASE

GOLF'S MOMENT OF TRUTH

Discover which release is best for your swing.

written by
JIM HARDY

Copyright © 2016 by Jim Hardy

All rights reserved. No part of this publication may be reproduced, distributed, or transmitted in any form or by any means, including photocopying, recording, or other electronic or mechanical methods, without the prior written permission of the publisher, except in the case of brief quotations embodied in critical reviews and certain other noncommercial uses permitted by copyright law. For permission requests, write to the publisher, addressed "Attention: Permissions Coordinator," at the address below.

Published by:
Plane Truth Productions
5929 Castlebar Lane
Plano, TX 75093
www.planetruthproductions.com
(281) 241-1100

Ordering Information:
Quantity sales. Special discounts are available on quantity purchases by corporations, associations, and others. For details, contact Plane Truth Productions Sales at the address above. Orders by U.S. trade bookstores and wholesalers, please contact the publisher.

Printed in the United States of America
Plane Truth Productions makes every effort to use acid-free, recycled paper.

ISBN 9780997316506

Library of Congress Control Number 2016937091

10 9 8 7 6 5 4 3 2 1
First Edition

Cover and Interior Design: James Zachman, Jr.
Publisher: Plane Truth Productions, LLC
Editor: MJ Rumminger

I dedicate this book to all the wonderful Plane Truth Certified professionals who daily show great desire to continue learning and improving. I draw tremendous energy from them to continue seeking better information and better ways to communicate it. And to Him who is Truth in His Matchless Grace.

TABLE OF CONTENTS

FOREWORD vi

ACKNOWLEDGMENT x

ONE | WHAT'S A RELEASE? 1

TWO | RELEASE HISTORY 19

THREE | PLANE AND PATH/ARC 27

FOUR | CLUBFACE AND TARGET, PLANE, PATH/ARC 37

FIVE | A GENERAL OVERVIEW OF THE TWO RELEASES 45

SIX | THE TWO RELEASES & PLANE, PATH,
WIDTH, ANGLE, CLUBFACE, ROC & SPEED 63

SEVEN | WHICH RELEASE IS BEST FOR YOUR
SWING PLANE? 89

EIGHT | EXECUTING THE LOP RELEASE, LOP
SHOT SHAPING & LOP MISTAKES 109

NINE | EXECUTING THE RIT RELEASE, RIT
SHOT SHAPING & RIT MISTAKES 139

TEN | SWING PHOTOS & DRILLS 191

FOREWORD

How many times have you wondered how a certain golfer with a seemingly horrible swing can hit it so good? Conversely you certainly have noticed and found confusing how another golfer with a "to die for" beautiful swing suddenly hits the ball all over the lot with no control whatsoever. All golfers encounter the struggle to not only hit good shots but to also be repetitive. One day we "have it" and the next day we "can't find it". Golf truly presents us with what seems a life time pursuit to unravel its mysteries. It certainly has been that way for me. As a player and as an instructor I've daily pursed the answers to the game and better ways to communicate them. You could safely say without overstating it that this has been my life's work; to come up with practical, simple, easily understood solutions that address golf's difficulty and that work. I want results and I want them to be immediate, not in three weeks or six months. I want them on the next ball or certainly in the next few balls. If the solution is correct and is simple to understand as well as easily put into your swing then you should get results. It's honestly that simple. If you're not improving either you didn't understand the information or you just didn't execute it that time or the information is wrong….simple.

Steve Jobs spoke to exactly this problem and solution issue when asked what philosophy drives Apple that results in the superior products they invent. He talked about his belief that there are three evolutionary steps that great solutions go through.

> "When you start looking at a problem, it seems really simple – because you don't understand its complexity. And your solutions are way too oversimplified, and they don't work. Then you get into the problem and you see it's really complicated. And you come up with

all these convoluted solutions. That's where most people stop, and the solutions tend to work for a while. But the really great person will keep going and find the key underlying principle of the problem and sort of come full circle with a beautiful, elegant solution that works."

It is exactly that final solution to the many problems we encounter in golf that I have always sought. I must admit to often becoming trapped in the evolutionary process Jobs describes. I've failed when the solution didn't adequately address the problem and I've suffered through such highly complex ideas that they were not practical or universally understandable. In each of my books I've tried to present a simple, elegant, workable solution to different golf problems. In my first book, *Plane Truth for Golfers,* I dealt with swing shape. In the second book, *Master Class* I gave swing shape lessons based upon ball flight misses. My third book, *Solid Contact,* explained the Plus and Minus System that allows golfers to easily fix any ball flight misses by adjusting their impact not by overhauling their swing. It is my hope you will find in this book on golf's releases simple answers that can be clearly grasped and easily implemented. The purpose of this book is to teach you how to achieve an improved club delivery that produces more power, accuracy and consistency.

Too much of what we hear of golf instruction is either way too simple or way too complex. It's either just another tip or the instruction is so clouded in scientific language that you need an advanced degree and a Crackerjack decoder ring to understand it. This book will completely explain club delivery and will teach you there are two very opposite ways to do it. Both are in the Hall of Fame and you'll learn which release belongs in your game and how to correctly execute it. You'll learn some scientific information on just why even the best players have bouts of hitting the ball poorly even though their swings do not change from shot to shot. One thing I will promise is you won't be bogged down with language you don't understand, or information that doesn't easily relate to results. We both want results and the clearer I communicate the information to you the sooner the results are achieved.

In closing this Foreword and opening the book to you I want you to know this is a work of a lifetime. There are several new discoveries to golf in this book that are exciting. There are several "myth busters" presented that burst many of the hallowed beliefs that are held as sacred in golf. I can totally assure you that everything I present in this book works. I've proven it over and over with my students' results; from Tour professionals to average golfers. Because what I say in this book is true, I only use a limited number of photos of myself and instead use photos of some of the greatest golfers to ever play this game to drive home my points. I want you to see and believe it, not just from me, but from seeing them as well. I earnestly hope this book improves your game and makes golf even more enjoyable.

Jim Hardy
December 31, 2015

ACKNOWLEDGMENT

Nearly all acknowledgements for this book begin and end with my Plane Truth Golf partners, Chris O'Connell and Mike Crisanti. Without their help and encouragement this book would not have happened.

Chris labored days gathering and selecting the wonderful photos in this book. He is my fellow explorer in golf's laboratory and many of the ideas presented he played a huge role in bringing them to fruition. Not too many days ever go by without the two of us talking about recent results and ideas for how to achieve what we want more quickly or more easily. We often laugh about the very old quiz show, Name That Tune, where contestants try to name a tune by hearing the fewest notes. That's our contest….to get golfers to fully comprehend and successfully execute a golf swing solution that results in a great impact and ball flight….with the simplest lesson. That's exactly what one of my instructors, Harvey Penick was famous for doing. The same goes for John Jacobs, another of my mentors. In fact I'd say all great instructors have that ability and Chris is no exception. He's one of the game's great instructors and I'd be lost without his friendship and counsel.

Mike is Plane Truth Golf's rock. He steadily moves Chris and me forward bringing our ideas into action through books, videos, training devices, educational training programs, web and internet opportunities. Under his direction we have flourished as a training and educational company for golf professionals worldwide. We will soon reach all levels of golfers through internet based educational opportunities that have never been presented before. It was his push to see this book published as a beautiful, thorough book on golf's releases that made it possible. Chris and I may be the idea guys but Mike is the brawn behind getting it done. Thanks to both of you.

My thanks to Jim A. Hardy, better known as YBL (younger and better looking) for all your help in the time line organizing, photo shoots, editing and just the everyday encouragement that comes so natural from you. You are a positive force in the world and a great friend to so many who need your help and wisdom.

To Bernie Najar who helps "prove out" my information with his wonderful technical tools and knowledge…my thanks for all your help. Bernie is a great instructor who supplied this book with many of the wonderful photos. His desire to learn and to thoroughly examine any information in the most scientific tests has proven invaluable collaboration for this book.

Special thanks to Terry Rowles and GolfswingHD for allowing us to use their extensive swing libraries. Also thank you to Andy Traynor, Joe Plecker, bauercti, gaspsys, Historic Golf Photos, and VisionsinGolf. Your contributions will allow the reader to see photos of the greatest golfers in the game implementing one of the two releases presented in this book. Thank you.

My thanks to Ken Lieberman whose photos of me illustrating the technical aspects of the releases help make it very clear exactly what the text is attempting to convey. Thank you to Mary Jane Rumminger who did a superb job of editing my text so it reads easily and correctly without any loss of my intent. You did a terrific job. The books layout and design was the hard work of James Zachman and I cannot thank him enough or give him high enough praise. This is a beautiful book that is readable and he is the person most responsible for that.

Finally, I want to acknowledge and thank my number one guinea pig that has suffered through all my experiments….my wonderful wife Marilyn. She is a terrific athlete and plus 2 handicap golfer. Anytime I would advance an idea to the point where I needed to see it live, in real time and in three dimensions, I would ask her to try it. She always did no matter how dubious some of the ideas were. She has been such a good sport to do it so I could "see" it and make adjustments that you just can't do with video. I'd guess for every good idea there were at least twenty five that were either completely wrong or certainly needed more thought. She's lived the efforts to discover this book's information and to get it right for 27 ½ years… I love you.

CHAPTER ONE

WHAT'S A RELEASE?

ONE | WHAT'S A RELEASE?

The release is undoubtedly the most important part of the golf swing, and it is the subject of this entire book. Right here at the beginning I want to point out the reason for this book: There is not just one way to release the club in the full golf swing. In fact there are two major categories of full swing releases. These two categories are both found in the Hall of Fame. They are not just different from one another—they are opposites. One release type belongs in your swing and the other absolutely does not. The purpose of this book is to fully explain both releases, determine which release is right for you and teach you how to maximize the execution of your release.

With the correct release type in your swing you will play your best golf every day. With the wrong one, you will suffer through the inconsistencies of great golf hand in hand with mediocre to terrible golf. The idea of two categories of release has been hinted at throughout golf's history. But with this book, for the first time these two opposite releases will be explained, detailed and taught to you. You will understand how to execute each one and be able to decide which one belongs in your swing. It's the "secret" you've been searching for all your golfing life.

The release is the heartbeat, brains and soul of the swing. In fact you could have a 100% biomechanically correct golf swing yet struggle if your release is flawed. On the other hand if you have a technically sound release it will overcome some biomechanical flaws and still produce splendid ball striking. Once you've discovered your release you'll become more powerful, more accurate and more repetitive than you ever dreamed. By controlling impact, you will possess the essence of the golf swing. To paraphrase my great mentor, John Jacobs, "The sole purpose of the golf swing is to produce a correct, repetitive impact."

Golf is a game of power and accuracy. It's a beautiful blend of both. There are a number of elements in the swing that contribute to a golfer's power and accuracy. But in the final analysis it's that part of a golfer's swing, coming into and through impact—we call it the release—that adds to and transmits the golfer's potential power to the ball. And it's the release that also largely determines the accuracy. Furthermore, it's the release that determines a golfer's ability to be repetitive with both his power and his accuracy. So to say the release area of the swing is important would be a great understatement. Ball control and power define the separation between poor golf and championship golf. The player who can predict his shot's outcome is the consummate shotmaker. That's ball control. To combine that shotmaking with power is golf's ultimate challenge. The release is vital to tackling that challenge, and it's one of the most misunderstood, controversial and highly debated elements of the golf swing.

To further understand just how important the release is, noted instructor and my great friend and colleague, Chris O'Connell, has been quoted as saying: "The release is everything—all the rest is just window dressing." Even Ben Hogan, in a conversation with David Frost reported in Golf Magazine and also verified to me by David, commented on the importance of the club's delivery. Frost had asked Hogan if he could give him any advice on the backswing. After a pause, Hogan answered, "Sonny, you don't hit the ball with your backswing." I've always loved that response because it hits dead in the heart of golf.

I'm not saying, nor do I believe Hogan meant, that the backswing is totally unimportant. But if your backswing is reasonable then get to work on what is important. The backswing does not have to be perfect. Nor does it have to be classic, beautiful or even very good. A great backswing does not ensure great hitting. One can have a perfect backswing and still hit the ball poorly. If it's just reasonably good, that's good enough. If this were not true, how in the world could you explain the phenomenal success of such players as Bubba Watson, Jim Furyk, Sergio Garcia, Lee Trevino, Matt Kuchar and Miller Barber, to name just a few great players with unorthodox or "not so pretty" backswings? Even Jack Nicklaus and Fred Couples have less than classic ones if you look at their "flying right elbows."

Because of his unorthodox backswing, I doubt if anyone ever goes up to Jim Furyk and asks him who his teacher is because they sure want to learn to swing like he does. People don't do that because they've been sold a bill of worthless goods on what's important. Most golfers think pretty is good, or classic is good or even having both would be much better. It's a shame, because they should ask Jim for his instructor's name and number. They should learn to deliver the clubhead to the ball, to release it just like Jim Furyk because he does it perfectly. Somewhere along the line Jim, and all the others above, plus countless other champions, realized or were taught just what was important. It's the release. "Sonny, you don't hit the ball with your backswing."

To understand the release in a golf swing let's start at the beginning. A dictionary definition of "release" as a verb is: "to free from anything that restrains, fastens, etc; such as to release a catapult." I like that definition very much. The release of the golf club in a swing is very much like a catapult in that the golfer is catapulting the clubhead through the ball. The catapult is a highly loaded lever and when the pressure is released on the catapult it moves with ferocious speed. The golf club is a lever with your hands/wrists at the fulcrum point. Equally, your arms can be viewed as levers with the fulcrum points at the elbows and shoulders. So like the catapult, your arms and club when loaded and then released swing through the air with ferocious speed. As a noun, release is defined as "liberation from anything that restrains or fastens." Notice that regardless of whether release is used as a verb or a noun, both definitions identify freedom/liberation as integral to the meaning of release.

The more freedom in the release, the more powerful and effective the release becomes. Tension, blocking and overcontrolling are all killers of the release.

When does the release begin and end? The release "zone" in the golf swing begins at that point in the downswing when the arms are somewhat parallel to the ground and continues to the point in the follow through when once again the arms are somewhat parallel to the ground. This is approximately waist high to waist high *(FIG. 1.1). The release involves the entire motion of the swing—the body, arms and club—throughout that zone. Let's look at some of the general characteristics of the swing during the release zone to further understand the definition of a correct golf release. Each characteristic is presented here in general terms. Some will be further discussed in far greater detail in later chapters. For simplicity and clarity (and please forgive me all of you left-handed golfers) any time I describe the release or how to do it I will use a golfer playing with right-handed clubs for my model. So instead of referring to the "lead arm" or the "trail arm" in the swing I shall just call it the left arm or the right arm.

While on the subject of simplicity, I'll also ask you ladies to please forgive my use of "he/him/his" for all third-person pronouns.

General Release Characteristics

ONE | CLUB PLANE

The clubhead and shaft move on a plane that is incanted upward and inward from the target line. The plane of the release varies greatly, depending upon the overall plane of the swing. That variance can be as great as a 15-degree difference between a flat plane *(FIG. 1.2) and an upright plane *(FIG. 1.3).

*FIG. 1.1

The release "zone" starts in the downswing when the arms are parallel to the ground and extends through impact to a point in the follow through where the arms are again parallel to the ground.

*FIG. 1.2

Flat release zone plane

*FIG. 1.3

Upright release zone plane

TWO | CLUBHEAD PATH

The path the clubhead takes when looking from directly overhead as it swings downward and outward along the plane towards the ball is an arc from inside the target line going outward towards the ball. The flatter the plane *(FIG. 1.4) the more exaggerated the arc and conversely the more upright the plane *(FIG. 1.5) the more gentle the arc. The path at impact is tangent to the target line for only a brief moment as it hits the ball. Then as the club starts its movement up the plane, the arc of the clubhead moves away from the target line in a fairly close mirror image of the downswing arc. The arc through the release zone can be described as from inside the target line to the target line and then back to the inside of the target line or simply, "in-to-in."

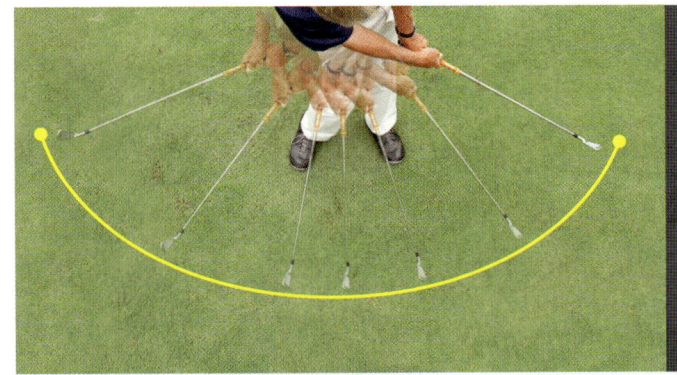

***FIG. 1.4**

Flat plane overhead arc

***FIG. 1.5**

Upright plane overhead arc

THREE | CLUBHEAD

The clubhead while moving on the in-to-in path is also moving, or more correctly stated, is being released, from the right side of the club's handle to the left side of the club's handle. While this release is happening the clubhead is moving downward, then somewhat level and then upward as it moves along the plane *(FIG. 1.6). This down and up movement creates a clubhead angle that corresponds to the downward or upward part of the plane.

FOUR | CLUBHEAD ANGLE

As a golf ball is positioned either more forward in the golfer's stance towards the target or more backward away from the target, the resulting clubhead angle of attack changes if the swing remains on plane. The more forward position results in a more upward blow to the ball. This is referred to as a shallow angle of attack; a more backward position will result in a more downward angle into the ball, or a steeper angle of attack.

*FIG. 1.6

The downward and upward view of the downswing and follow through arc.

FIVE | CLUBHEAD PATH/ARC

As the golf ball is played farther back in the stance, the part of the arc or path the clubhead is on when it hits the ball will be oriented to the target line as more from inside the target line and will swing in a direction oriented more to the right of the target line. This is often referred to as hitting "more from the inside," or sometimes referred to as hitting "inside out" *(FIG. 1.7). Conversely, a ball positioned forward in the stance will be hit when the clubhead is moving upward and away from the target line—when the arc or path is oriented to the left of the target line *(FIG. 1.8). This is often referred to as hitting "back to the inside" or "more across the ball" or sometimes referred to as "cutting across the ball" or even "outside in."

SIX | CLUBFACE & TARGET

Understanding what is happening to the clubface during the release is vital. The clubface RELATIVE TO THE GOLFER'S TARGET is undergoing a profound change during the release. The clubface is moving from wide open to the target as it enters the start of the release zone to closed to the target as it exits the zone. That clubface change can be as much as much as 180 degrees or even considerably more.

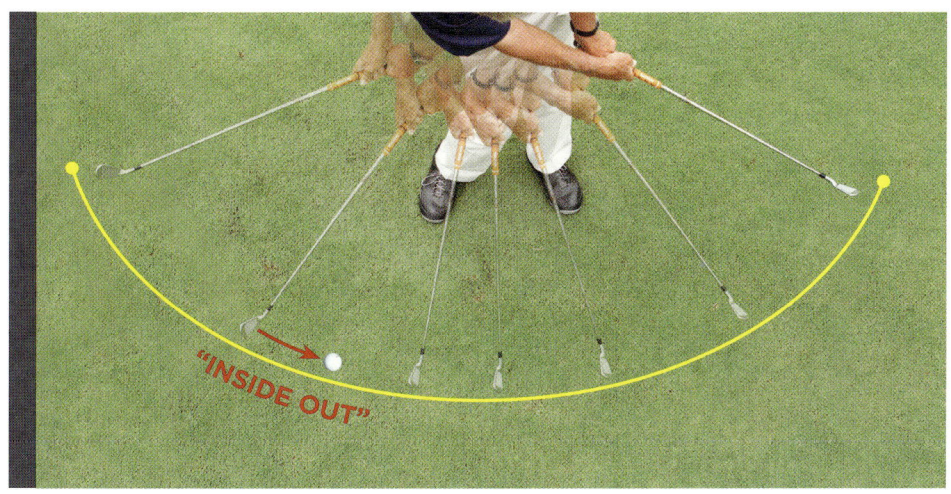

***FIG. 1.7**

Ball back in stance creates an inside out path relative to the target.

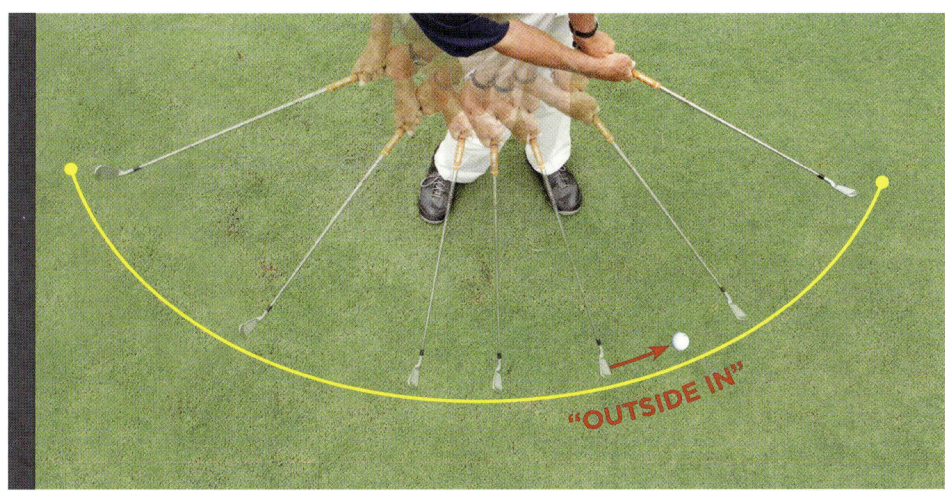

***FIG. 1.8**

Ball forward in stance creates an outside in path relative to the target.

SEVEN | CLUBFACE & PATH/ARC

The clubface as it closes relative to the target has several options relative to the path/arc, depending on the type of release employed. The variance between releases can be as great as one release having a clubface fairly square to the path/arc throughout the release zone while another could have the clubface 90 degrees or even more open to the path/arc and then rapidly becoming 90 degrees or more closed to the arc. This phenomenon of the great open-and-then-closed differences between how the clubface is positioned relative to the path/arc in the release zone I will refer to as the "RATE OF CLOSURE" or ROC. The reason I use the term ROC to describe the clubface closure in relation to the path/arc is because that relationship is vital to understanding straight shots and curving shots. The clubface relative to the target is only valuable in putting where we don't have a ball flight and the ball primarily responds to the clubface. In shot making the clubface to the target relationship is fairly worthless while the clubface relationship to the path/arc is extremely important. So again I'll repeat, the term ROC as I'll use it is the RATE OF CLUBFACE CLOSURE during the release zone in relation to the PATH/ARC. Some releases have a very slow ROC *(FIG. 1.9) in that they are "square to the path/arc" for a long time in the zone while other releases have a very high ROC *(FIG. 1.10) because the clubface is "square to the path/arc" for only a very short period of time. The clubface in those releases is either open to the path/arc or closed to the path/arc, and when it goes from open to closed it does so very rapidly.

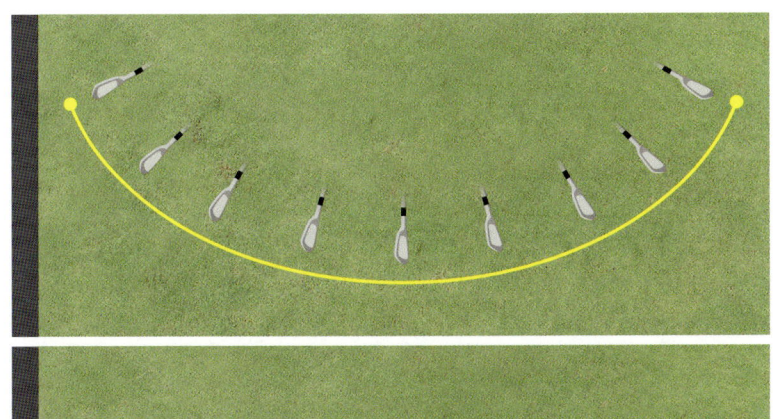

FIG. 1.9

This is a slow ROC with the clubface square to the path for a fairly long time.

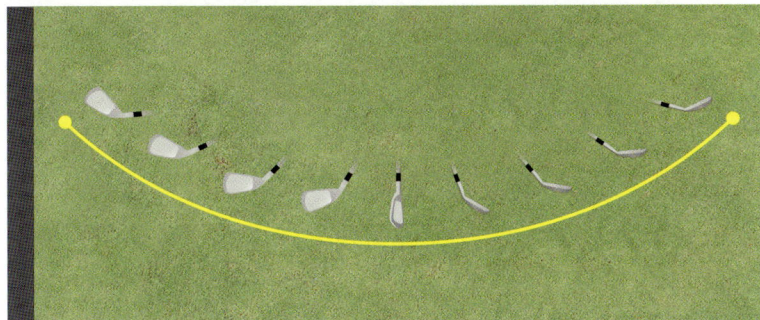

FIG. 1.10

This is a high ROC with the clubface moving open to closed to the path quickly.

EIGHT | CLUBFACE, ANGLE & BALL

One element of the release is to control how the clubface strikes the ball. To hit solid shots the clubface must hit the back of the ball (not the sides of the ball) with an appropriate angle to hit the particular club or shot the player is attempting. Each club in general requires a slightly different angle of attack. The longest clubs require the most shallow or level angle and the shortest usually require the steepest or most downward angle. This is because as the shaft gets longer it sits at address on a flatter angle to the ground. The short irons are the shortest clubs and sit at address in the most upright angle to the ground. These address factors, dictated by the length of each club, also dictate the plane a club will ideally swing on and the angle at which it returns to the ball. The longer the club, the flatter the plane and the shallower the angle of hit will be. Conversely, the shorter the club, the more upright the plane and the steeper the angle of hit will be. In addition to hitting the back of the ball, the golfer is attempting during the release to hit the ball in the center or "sweet spot" of the clubface.

NINE | CLUBFACE, PATH/ARC & BALL

To play a straight shot, the clubface must be square to the path at impact and hit in the middle of the clubface. To play a straight ball at the target, you must accomplish these things plus have the path at impact pointed at the target. To play shots that curve require the player to have a clubface that IS NOT SQUARE to the path. A clubface that is closed to the path will hit a shot that curves either slightly or significantly to the left. That shot is termed a draw or hook. If the clubface is open to the path/arc it is termed a fade or slice. The amount of curvature either shot has depends on the amount/degree the clubface is not square to the path as well as the club's loft. The more the clubhead is closed or open to the path and/or the club has little loft the greater the curvature. Conversely, the less the clubface is closed or open to the path/arc and/or the club is more lofted, the less the curvature. Hitting off center can also affect curvature especially when hitting a hybrid, fairway metal or driver. Assuming a reasonably square clubface, a ball hit in the heel of the club will increase the ball's curve to the right, and a strike on the toe will increase the ball's curve to the left.

TEN | PLANE ARM

When standing to the golfer's right on the target line looking down range in what is referred to as a down-the-line position, the plane arm is the arm parallel to the plane as the swing progresses through the release zone, it is the arm that the clubshaft is aligned with and is often the outside arm, meaning the arm closest to the target line. As the swing enters the zone, the plane arm is usually the left arm. It is the arm that is pointed down the plane at the target line and the clubshaft is aligned with the left arm *(FIG. 1.11). At some point during the release the plane arm is going to shift to the right arm and it will be the right arm that the clubshaft is aligned with. The exact place/time when this exchange happens varies greatly between the two releases and is the primary reason for the differing ROC's between the releases.

Fig. 1.11

Entering the zone the plane arm is the left arm.

ELEVEN | SPEED

The release is a source of great speed in the swing. It's the last chance to add more speed by the action of the hands and arms accelerating the shaft and clubhead through the release zone. Although great speed is attained through the release, certainly not all clubhead speed is attributable to the release. But all clubhead speed is applied and coordinated through the release. If the release is incorrect, regardless of the potential speed that has been developed, that speed will not be delivered to either the clubhead or into the back of the ball. As noted above, think of the release as the swing's catapult. Coming into the release zone you have tremendous potential for speed that has been built up. That speed must be liberated, set free, and in doing so must be released in such a fashion that will be applied correctly to the ball. For even if we release tremendous speed, if it is not applied squarely into the back of the ball, hitting the center of the clubface, on a correct path and clubface alignment with an angle suitable to the club employed—that speed is useless. In fact, that sentence is a pretty good start for defining the purpose of the release. Let's summarize all the elements we've looked at and come up with a comprehensive release definition.

The release is a movement of the golf club primarily by the use of the hands, wrists and arms that occurs in a downswing and follow through "release zone" from waist high to waist high. Ideally it moves the clubshaft/clubhead downward and outward square into the back of the ball and then upward and inward, all the while swinging on a plane incanted upward and inward from the target line. It closes the clubface relative to the target throughout the zone, allows the plane arms to switch, and delivers the clubhead and the clubface on a correct path and face alignment, with an angle of attack suitable for the shot while accelerating the clubhead from the right side of the club's handle to its left side.

WOW—If you'll pardon me that was quite a mouthful. Our definition seems long, a little complicated and maybe cumbersome, but that's because there are a lot of things happening during the release. We are doing several things to produce a correct release and the release itself is attempting to accomplish a number of things. The good news is we are going to tackle these release elements one at a time so we can accomplish a complete understanding of them. After that we will examine the two distinctly different, actually quite opposite releases and how to produce them. First though let's take a look at these two methods as they have been described throughout golf's history.

TWO | RELEASE HISTORY

Throughout the history of golf, players as well as instructors have discussed, debated and argued about not just the swing but its many components. The release and how to do it has certainly been a part of those dialogues. It has generated its share of rigid beliefs whose proponents have declared their way is the only way to properly deliver the club into the ball. In fact, this is still very true today. Not a month goes by without a new article coming out that promises to cure your slice and add at least 25 yards to your average shot. There's a lot of information out there and most of it falls into two categories. One category is just foolish information and not only won't help your game, it will actually harm it. The other category is full of correct information. The problem with the correct category is about half the pieces of information are completely contradictory to the other half. This has always been the case. So how can contradictory information on the same subject all be correct? There's a simple answer to that seemingly confusing question. If it's all correct but around half of it stands in contradiction to the other half, there must be two general ways to release the golf club. As noted earlier, these contradictory views of the release have been with us for a very long time. Let's look at some of these opposing ideas on the release.

Early on, particularly in the era of the small ball before the current size golf ball was universally adopted, the release was strictly a hands dominated wristy effort. The outfits that golfers wore were very restrictive with suit type jackets, starched collars, ties and, in particular, suspenders or braces as they were often called. This golfing attire did not allow for a great deal of athletic movement and severely limited the arm swing and a great deal of the body pivot. The body pivot was mostly performed by exaggerated footwork. The use of the arms to help with the swinging of the club was certainly restricted by the shirts, ties, jackets and suspenders. The release was pretty much reduced to a "flicking" movement of the wrists as the footwork moved the body pivot into and past impact. It was the advent of both the big ball and modern golf clothing that really brought about the release movements as we know them today.

Several noted players and instructors who hit the scene about that time started observing and recording how great players were often doing very different things during the release. The great British champion, Henry Cotton, wrote extensively about various releases he had observed. He was a golf pioneer who used photography to show these different releases, and gave them names such as: the hinge/slap, the forearm rotation and the push. One of golf's great instructors from just after WW1 through the middle of the last century, Ernest Jones, wrote about swinging the clubhead through the release zone and never "leveraging" the club. Although he recognized some golfers did use a leverage type of club delivery, he strongly despised it and did not think it was either desirable or reliable.

As I grew up in the 60s, I heard Byron Nelson as well as many other golf notables on television and in instructional articles refer to golfers as "swingers" or "hitters." I certainly didn't know what constituted either but was determined to experiment with both methods. On a given day I would try being smooth and "swing-like" and on the next day tried to hit at the ball as hard as I could. It was when I was in college that I started to hear a couple of terms different from swingers or hitters. Now they were being called "pullers" or "throwers." I remember hearing about the great, flamboyant long hitter, Mike Austin, who at age 59 hit the longest drive ever recorded in an official tournament and on flat land— 516 yards. That certainly caught my attention and I immediately sought out everything I could about him. He was an absolute believer in "throwing" the club. He wanted to shift his weight to begin the downswing and then throw the club with his right hand as hard and as fast as he could. He was so against "pulling" that he produced a film showing him hitting a driver with a rope tied around the end of the grip and looped around a bent left elbow which he held tight to his chest. The only hand on the club was his right hand and he demonstrated that starting down he could not pull on the club in his downswing because his left arm wasn't attached to the club, only the rope and his right hand were attached. So the only way he could actually move the club was by throwing it with his right hand and arm. Another long hitting thrower, reigning world long drive champ Jeff Flagg in the May 2015 issue of Golf Digest was asked, "What are you thinking about when you swing?" His response was; "My only real thought is, right hand and arm drive the swing. That's it. I'm literally trying to make a sidearm throwing motion – like a 3-6-3 double play in baseball. If more golfers swung with the same motion, as if they were skipping stones, they'd pound the ball."

It wasn't long after I discovered Mike Austin and his throwing delivery that Jim Flick began to make his name as a noteworthy instructor with such books as *The Square-to-Square Golf Swing,* and he talked about pulling with the left arm. He allowed that some people did throw the club but he much preferred pulling it. He even developed a drill he used for a long time in his Golf Digest Schools where he would ask students to swing the club with only their left arms and then when they put their right hands on the club, to grip very lightly with the right. He then would have them remove the right hand from the club immediately after impact to increase the sensation of swinging the club entirely through with the left arm.

These contradictory release methods of "leverage the club vs. swing the clubhead," "swingers vs. hitters" and "pullers vs throwers" were also joined by famous golfers such as Ben Hogan, who said emphatically that he used his right hand to release the club as soon and as fast as he could. In fact he said he used it right from the start of the downswing and wished he had two right hands (I assume he meant instead of one right hand and one left hand). A few years later he changed his mind and stated that he wished he had three right hands. In Kris Tschetter's book, *Mr. Hogan, The Man I Knew*, she went into some detail about how much Hogan wanted her to hit the ball as hard as she could with her right hand. In fact she couldn't hit it too hard with the right hand.

Meanwhile, countless other great professionals and instructors have written books on the vital importance of pulling down with the left hand and arm while never allowing the right to "take over." Such terms as "forward leaning shaft" and "late hit" started to populate our golf terminology in stark contrast to golfers such as Jack Nicklaus, who insisted he tried to start uncocking his wrists at the start of the downswing. Hall of Fame instructor Eddie Merrins's method of "Swing the Handle" stood in stark contrast to Ernest Jones's method of "Swing the Clubhead."

So you can clearly see, the delivery of the club through the ball—the release—has been hotly debated throughout golf's history. For a long time I thought one of these camps had to be more correct than the other. As I played through my college golf and then onto the PGA Tour I too noticed firsthand that great golfers seemed to be delivering the club into and through the ball very differently. My conclusion was that apparently we were all playing a very schizophrenic game, and there was certainly more than one totally correct way to do it.

Although I wasn't aware of it at the time, this conclusion that there must be more than one way to correctly hit the ball shaped my life as an instructor. My first book, *The Plane Truth for Golfers,* details two distinctly different full swing categories, "One Plane" or "Two Plane," into which all swings fall regardless of whether the golfer is a high handicapper or in the Hall of Fame. For instance a high handicapper and a Hall of Famer might both have swings in the One Plane category but clearly one of them doesn't have a very good One Plane swing and the other player obviously does. This is also true of swings in the Two Plane category. Defining two different categories of swings separates all the full swing contradictions that we hear every day into information that works best when employed in one swing category or another.

Through this book on the release, I intend to clear up the contradictions that apply to that critical portion of the swing. There are two major categories of release and as you've already had a peek into them, you have an idea of just how extraordinarily different they are. Yet in all truthfulness, you haven't even scratched the surface of how different.

But before we dive into the releases—what they are, how they work, which one is best for your swing and how to correctly execute them—we have more preparatory ground to cover. First off, since both the releases move the club along a plane, we need to be clear about exactly what constitutes a golfer's plane.

CHAPTER THREE

PLANE & PATH/ARC

THREE | PLANE AND PATH/ARC

The term "plane" as it relates to golf is highly overused and poorly understood. A golfer's plane is simply a three dimensional surface that illustrates where the arms and the club move through space during a swing. A correct plane is one that is oriented to the golf ball and has two elements. In addition the plane has a direction that may or may not be oriented at the target.

The two elements that make up a plane are separately determined by 1) the nature of how we play golf and 2) where the ball is located. First let's deal with the element that relates to the nature of golf. All endeavors where an object is moved, shot, thrown, kicked, heaved, etc., are divided into two types of games: on-line games and side-on games. On-line sports are where you stand on the target line, facing your target. Think of croquet, softball pitching, overhand baseball throwing, shooting pool, throwing horseshoes, throwing darts, throwing a javelin, straight-on kicking, shuffleboard and curling to name a few. What all these games have in common, regardless of whether the motion is underhand, overhand or somewhere in between, is that the motion is predominately in a straight line—straight back and straight through.

Side-on games are where we find golf, baseball hitting, throwing a discus, hockey, side-on kicking in soccer and football, certain forehand and backhand shots in tennis and ping pong, and the track and field hammer throw. All these sports, because you stand to the side or are "side-on" to the target line, are circular in nature. Therefore <u>one element of a plane is a circular movement</u>. This is contrary to theories that you are supposed to swing the club straight at the target, or straight down the target line as far as possible. That is just not the case. You move in a straight line in on-line games. In side-on games you must move in a circular manner. If you are "on plane" and if you wish to hit solid, powerful and repetitive golf shots then you must have a circular element to your swing plane. That's a fact.

The second element that makes up a plane considers the fact the ball is located on the ground. With side-on sports where the ball is not located on the ground, but say between mid thigh and shoulder high, the plane would be circular but fairly level to the ground. A discus throw, along with baseball hitting, hammer throw and certain tennis shots have this type of plane—circular and fairly level to the ground. Since golf, some tennis shots, side-on kicking in soccer and football and most hockey shots have the object to be moved on the ground, their planes must have a vertical element in it. So the second element in a plane is an up and down element that deals with the ball on the ground.

Fig. 3.1

The plane is a blend of vertical and horizontal forces.

Putting these two elements together forms a golf plane. It's a circular motion that is oriented to the ground. A simple definition of the plane would be: "While the golfer is swinging upward in the backswing he is also swinging around, or while he is swinging around he is swinging upward. It is a blend of vertical up along with horizontal around forces *(FIG. 3.1). In the downswing, while swinging down he is also swinging back around in front of him and then in the follow through while swinging up again, he is also swinging back around again." More simply stated the golfer while swinging up, down and up is also swinging around in a circular fashion or while swinging around in a circular fashion the golfer is also at the same time swinging up and down.

The plane also has a direction in relation to the target. A "correct" or "neutral" plane is one that is aimed at the target. A plane aimed to the right of the target is commonly called inside-out *(FIG. 3.2) and a plane aimed left of the target is often referred to as out-to-in *(FIG. 3.3)—more on this in a moment. Ben Hogan was a pioneer in understanding and writing about the plane. He felt strongly about the plane's importance. In fact he states in his book, Five Lessons,

*FIG. 3.2

Inside-out plane direction

*FIG. 3.3

Outside-in plane direction

the Modern Fundamentals of Golf, that it wasn't until he could "see" his plane that he finally knew he could play good golf every day. Interestingly, as you'll see later, the plane he drew did not match his swing and release type. He was correct however in stating he swung under the plane he had drawn.

Every correct plane is circular, but not every plane is angled upward and inward at the same angle. In fact there is a fairly large difference between the plane angles of great golfers within the Hall of Fame. Upright planes *(FIG. 3.4) like the ones Jack Nicklaus and Tom Watson swung on are considerably more upward angled from the target line than say the much flatter planes *(FIG. 3.5) Ben Hogan and Gary Player swung on. Modern players who swing on decidedly upright planes include Bubba Watson, Ian Poulter, Jason Day, Karrie Webb, Cristie Kerr, while the decidedly flatter plane players are Hunter Mahan, Sergio Garcia, Rory McIlroy, Rickie Fowler, and Matt Kuchar. I will discuss in detail during a later chapter the two distinctly different

*FIG. 3.4

Upright swing plane

*FIG. 3.5

Flat swing plane

ways the body and arms combine to form a plane. Additionally I will cover which release best suits or fits the way you have formed your plane. In this chapter my purpose simply is to establish in general terms an understanding of the plane.

Let's move on from the plane to a discussion of the path or arc. If the plane is a three dimensional surface that describes the motion of the arms and club during the swing, the path or arc is a one dimensional curved line that illustrates the line the clubhead moves on during the swing. The path/arc is a depiction of that movement when viewed from directly above as the club moves along the golfer's plane during the swing. Since the subject of this book is the release, the portion of the clubhead's path/arc we will study occurs as the club moves from above waist high to just above waist high downward and outward along the plane in the downswing and then upward and inward in the follow through. As noted in Chapter One, a correct path is an arc and is commonly referred to as an "in-to-in" arc as it travels from inside the target line out to the ball and then back inward away from the target line again. This correct path is formed when the golfer's plane is correct and pointed somewhat at the target. If the golfer's plane is pointed to the right of the target the resulting path/arc will be inside-out instead of in-to-in. Conversely, if the plane is pointed to the left it will result in a path/arc that is outside-in.

An additional consideration of the plane's influence on the path/arc concerns the degree of the upward tilt of the plane. The more upright tilt of the plane, the more subtle or less dramatically curved is the path/arc when viewed from above. If the plane were totally vertical like a Ferris wheel, the club would still be swinging in a circular motion but the path/arc of the clubhead as it moved along that plane, when viewed from directly above, would be a straight line. Conversely if the plane were flat along the ground like a merry-go-round the path/arc would be a perfect circle. Since the golfer's plane is incanted (angled upward and inward), when the club swings in a circular motion along it the path/arc described is neither a perfect circle nor a straight line. It is better described as a section of an oval. The more upright the plane the less dramatic the arc, while the flatter the plane the more dramatic is the arc's curvature.

The last consideration of the relationship of the plane to the path/arc is best understood if, instead of viewing the path/arc from its traditional vantage point of directly above, it is viewed while facing the front of the golfer. That view we call face-on. From here you can notice the width of the swing. From the one dimensional overhead view of the path/arc you see the in-to-in nature of the swing. From the one dimensional face-on view you see the swing shape from a width perspective. Here you see the clubhead swing down from the

Fig. 3.6

A wide more "U" like swing bottom.

Fig. 3.7

A narrow more "V" like swing bottom.

top of the backswing to the ground. At this point, before the clubhead starts swinging back up again you can notice just how long the clubhead stays near or somewhat tangent to the ground. The longer this "flat spot" where the club stays fairly near the ground the more we refer to the swing bottom as having width. It is a wide or sweepy swing bottom, like a wide "U" *(FIG. 3.6). The less the swing stays tangent to the ground the more it is termed a narrow swing bottom, like a "V" *(FIG. 3.7). Wide swings are usually more forgiving but tend to hit the ball low—think Gary Player or Lee Trevino. Narrow swings while a little less forgiving certainly hit the ball higher—think Jack Nicklaus or Bubba Watson.

There are several factors that influence the swing bottom's width but primary among them is the swing plane; the more upright the plane the narrower the swing bottom and conversely the flatter the plane the wider the swing bottom. To illustrate this, imagine a big tractor tire standing fairly upright. In that position only a small part of the tire at the bottom is on or close to the ground and the tread quickly moves up from the ground on both sides. Now imagine the same tire lying almost on its side. In that position a lot of the bottom of the tire is on or close to the ground and the tread on both sides moves very gradually upward away from the ground. Now hopefully you can "see" the bottom of the swing and how in a general sense an upright plane is narrower, more V-like and a flatter plane is wider, more U-like.

We've examined the plane and how it influences the path/arc as well as the swing's width. Let's now look at how the clubface works in the release zone.

CHAPTER FOUR

CLUBFACE & TARGET,
PLANE, PATH/ARC

FOUR | CLUBFACE AND TARGET, PLANE, PATH/ARC

As mentioned in Chapter One the clubface in the downswing has two relationships. One relationship is to the target and the other is to the plane and or the path/arc. At address, the clubface, if held correctly, is square to the target and to the plane/path. Square simply means it is at right angles, or 90 degrees, to the target line, and the plane/path. As the golfer makes a backswing the clubface starts to open relative to the target because the club is moving on a circular path from in front of the golfer to behind him. Years ago, someone figured out if the golfer, while he made his backswing, tried to keep the clubface square to the plane/path he could not cock his hands in a powerful manner. The only way to cock the club powerfully as you form the backswing is to twist your wrists/forearms approximately 90 degrees at some point before you reach the top of the backswing. This twist of the wrists ends up opening the clubface to the plane/path approximately 90 degrees, assuming a neutral left-hand grip *(FIG. 4.1). Even with a strong left-hand grip the clubface will be open to the plane/path at the top but will be less than the 90-degree open position of the neutral grip. Interestingly enough, what we call square at the top is actually around 90 degrees open to both the target and the plane/path. Since the left arm at that point in the swing is the "plane arm" as discussed in Chapter One, the clubface at the top is also approximately 90 degrees open to the left arm.

As we swing down to around waist high, which is the start of the release zone, the clubface is still somewhere around 90 degrees open to the left arm, the target and the plane/path. As noted in Chapter One, a function of the release is to square the clubface into the back of the ball. On a straight shot, the release squares the clubface to the

***FIG. 4.1**

Left photo shows a clubface square to plane but non powerful arm and wrist cock position. Right photo shows a clubface open 90 degrees to plane but a powerful arm and wrist cock position.

Fig. 4.2

The clubface entering the zone is approximately 90 degrees open to the left arm, the target and the plane/path.

target, to the plane/path and to the plane arm either before or at the exact moment of impact. On hooks/draws the clubface at impact is released closed to the plane/path. It may or may not be square to the target depending on the ball's start line. Opposite to the hook/draw, with slices/fades the clubface at impact is open to the plane/path. Similarly it may or may not be open to the target, depending on the ball's start line. One thing is certain though, the clubface in the release zone starts out approximately 90 degrees open to the target, the plane/path and the left arm *(FIG. 4.2).

Now let's examine how the clubface works as it travels through the impact zone in the two different releases. It is dramatically different and since the clubface is in charge of ball control (one of our objectives) we need to thoroughly understand how the clubface reacts in the two releases.

In one category of release the clubface stays open to the plane arm, the target and the plane/path until just before impact. At that point it undergoes a fast-closing rotation where it is square to the plane/path for only a brief moment; that moment of "squareness" is so short it is measured in thousandths of a second—that's short and quick. Beyond or just past that moment of being square the clubface as it completes its journey through the release zone is closed to the target, the plane/path and the plane arm *(FIG. 4.3). The accompanying photos show this from a down the line perspective. In Chapter One on page 13, *(FIG. 1.10) there is an overhead perspective of a clubface going through rotation from open to the path and then closed to the path. The ROC (rate of closure) for that release is extremely high. You might think, why would I ever want a release that has such a high rate of ROC and is almost never square to my plane/path or my plane arm? Good question and the answer is that particular release can get you into the Hall of Fame if it fits your swing type and plane and you know how to make it work. Obviously there will be more to come on that.

The second kind of release starts out entering the release zone in somewhat the same position; the plane arm is the left arm, the clubface is approximately 90 degrees open to the target, to the plane arm and to the plane/path. It is however undergoing some immediate changes at around this point. The arm plane is dramatically changing

*FIG. 4.3

A high ROC where the clubface just before impact is 90 degrees open to the plane arm, the target and the plane/path and an instant after impact is 90 degrees closed.

from the left arm to the right arm, the clubface is also dramatically changing from open to square to the plane/path and the clubface is only slightly open to the target. From this point through the impact zone, the right arm remains the plane arm, the clubface remains square to the plane/path and the clubface gently squares and then gently closes to the target *(FIG. 4.4). The accompanying photos show this from a down the line perspective. In Chapter One on page 11, *(FIG. 1.9) there is an overhead perspective of a clubface while going from open to closed to the target is in fact square to the path for a long period while in the zone. Since the ROC is a relationship between the clubface and the path/arc, this release has a very low ROC. Since the clubface is square to where you are swinging (the plane/path) pretty much throughout the zone, the release has a very stable clubface. That means this release will hit straight shots or shots that only very

***FIG. 4.4**

A very low ROC where the clubface just before impact is square to the plane/path and an instant after impact is still square to the plane/path.

slightly curve. They may be slight pushes or pulls depending on the point on the arc the ball is located, but the shots will be mainly straight. So you say, that sounds good to me, I think I like that one better. Well it may be better for you and it may not be. Again, your swing type and plane will determine the best release fit for you. Just remember, both releases are used by champions and one of them will move you in that direction as well.

So in review: One release (High ROC) has the clubface open to the path/plane/arc, square for an instant, and then closed to the path/plane/arc. The other (Low ROC) has the clubface square to the path/plane/arc throughout the impact area. Both however have the clubface square to the target for only a very short period.

Chapter Five has a general overview of both releases, names them and focuses on their differences. Chapter Six reviews the releases in detail. Further chapters describe which release works best for your swing type and plane. In the chapters beyond we will teach you how to execute both releases and provide drills that help you quickly learn either type. Finally we'll show you photos of players using the releases. That's a lot to cover so let's get moving.

CHAPTER FIVE

A GENERAL OVERVIEW OF THE TWO RELEASES

FIVE | A GENERAL OVERVIEW OF THE TWO RELEASES

These next few chapters present the two releases in a way I often have cautioned my daughter when tackling difficult concepts: Proceed with continuous bite-sized portions rather than the entire mouthful at one time. Understanding the two releases requires some detail that could be overwhelming if not presented and comprehended one step at a time before moving on to the next piece. Let's start with a review of the historical names and a general overview of the two very different and nearly opposite releases.

The historical release names presented in Chapter Two are the basis for the general overview of the two releases plus I'm going to add a couple more; outward and inward. These names help give us a description of what's going on. So let's put them into two groups.

Group One release includes Leverage, Pullers, Hitters, Left Arm/Hand and Outward. Group Two includes Swing the Clubhead, Throwers, Swingers, Right Arm/Hand and Inward. You can already sense their opposite natures. To not get mixed up at any time during the rest of the book as well for simplicity, I'll refer to the

Group One release as Left/Outward/Pull or simply the LOP release and to the Group Two release as the Right/Inward/Throw as the RIT release. Also as we move from one aspect of the releases to another, I will present the details of each release together. I firmly believe when we can see their differences side by side we can better understand each one. It's when we can see the opposite nature of something that we can truly understand it. Without sour we don't fully understand sweet; as also with hot/cold, spring/fall, up/down, etc. So I ask, beg and implore you: To fully understand one release please read everything about the other as well. You may already think you know which release you should incorporate into your swing. You may say: "I pull with the left arm from the top; it's a key to my swing. I don't need to even bother with this throwing release." That would be a big mistake on your part. Read the whole book before you decide which release best suits your swing. Then go back and study those portions of the book that pertain to your chosen release. I promise you will have a far greater understanding of what your release is and how to do it if you first understand both of them.

Before we start looking into the releases I want to provide some terminology on how the wrist works. The wrist is a six-way joint *(fig. 5.1). It works in three different pairs. Those pairs in laymen's terms are 1) Throwing, 2) Twisting or Rotating and 3) Hinging or Cocking. The medical terms for them can be seen in the accompanying chart for the three groups, where Throwing is FLEXION and EXTENSION; Twisting or Rotating is PRONATION and SUPINATION; and Hinging is RADIAL DEVIATION and ULNAR DEVIATION. It's important you understand this terminology as I'll refer to these terms as well as to the laymen's terms for these wrist movements throughout the book.

General Overview...Release Zone to Impact:

As the golfer enters the impact zone the left arm is the plane arm as you can note it is pointed at the target line/ball. Also note when standing to the golfer's right on the target line looking down range, or what is referred to as a down-the-line position, there is a hole at this point between the positions of the left arm and the right arm in BOTH releases. You may note other differences in the photos as we move along but we'll get into those later. Right now focus on what is going to happen to that hole while the two releases move into and through impact. In both releases the hole disappears. It disappears because the plane arm changes from the left arm to the right arm. It is that exchange that closes the hole. In the LOP release the hole disappears because the left arm stays pretty much where it is as the PLANE ARM (with the clubshaft aligned with it) and the right arm

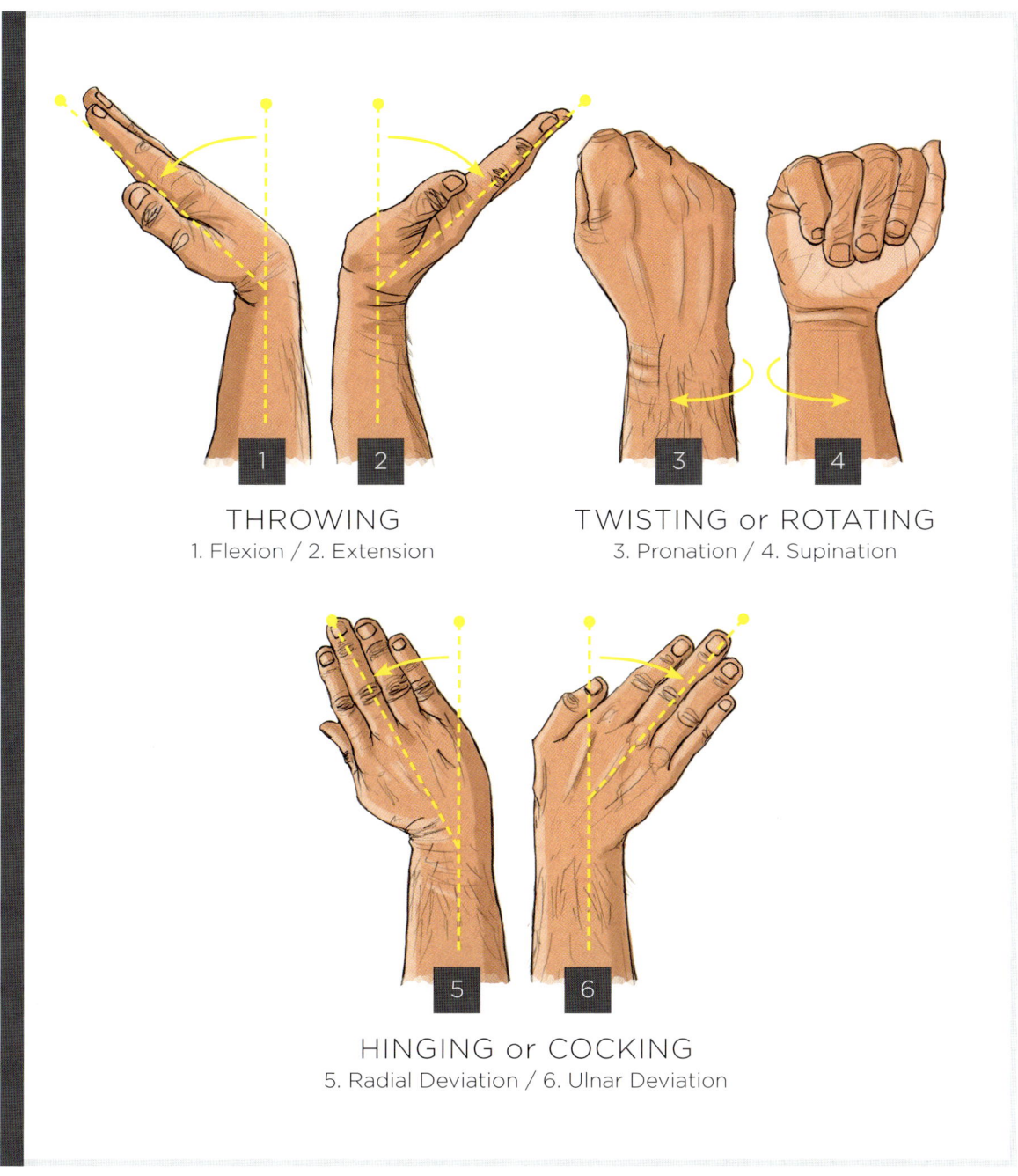

*FIG. 5.1

Wrist movement terminology.

moves OUTWARD to join it and become the plane arm *(FIG. 5.2). It is these two points I want to stress for the LOP release: The clubshaft is lined up with the LEFT ARM and the hole is closed due to the right arm's moving OUTWARD and becoming the plane arm. Both arms as the hole is closed are, for just a tiny moment in time, the plane arms, and as the swing moves on it's clearly the right arm that becomes the plane arm in the follow through.

In the RIT release notice how the hole between the arms disappears in exactly the opposite way. It disappears INWARD. Instead of the right arm moving outward to close the hole the <u>left arm move</u>s <u>downward and inward</u> to close it. The left arm gets out from in front of the right arm so the right arm can become the plane arm. Please notice the left arm does not point at the target line/ball. In fact it's pointing somewhere just beyond or at the golfer's toes. It's the right forearm that's pointing at the ball. The instant the release starts to happen as the RIT enters the release zone the CLUBSHAFT STARTS LINING UP WITH THE RIGHT FOREARM, the left arm is dropping downward and inward and the RIGHT forearm becomes the PLANE ARM as it points at the target line and ball before impact. It continues as the plane arm through impact and the follow through. It is these two points I want to stress for the RIT release: The clubshaft is lined up with the RIGHT FOREARM and the hole is closed due to the left arm's moving downward and INWARD, allowing the right arm to become the plane arm. It's vital you understand this general

*FIG. 5.2

Notice in the large photos on the left in both the upper (LOP release) and lower (RIT release) sequences a hole between the arms is present at the start of the impact zone. Now examine the upper LOP release sequence and notice how the hole in the arms closes outward. In the bottom RIT release sequence the hole in the arms closes exactly the opposite way. It now closes inward. It is this outward closing and inward closing difference I want to stress.

Fig. 5.3

The LOP after impact has the hole closed outward and the right arm the plane arm.

Fig. 5.4

The RIT after impact has the hole closed inward and the right arm the plane arm.

overview of the two releases and can see these major points. You also can understand why they are called Left Arm/Outward *(FIG. 5.3) or Right Arm/Inward *(FIG. 5.4) releases. We will deal with why and how the other names apply in a moment. But right now, please review the above material and photos on the left arm/outward and the right arm/inward natures of the two releases until you are perfectly clear.

Now let's move to the next step. Looking at the same down-the-line photos let's again examine the LOP release first. The left arm as it points at the target line is in a PULLING motion. In fact it has been in a pulling motion all the way from the start of the downswing. The more the left arm has been pulling the more passive a role the right arm has played. The right arm/hand must in the LOP release play a passive role from the start of the downswing all the way as it enters the release zone. Any active efforts during this part of the downswing with either the right arm or right hand will destroy the LOP release. As far as the motion of the arms go, getting from the top of the backswing down to the release zone must be all left hand/arm pull. I'll talk about the role of the body for the two releases later.

As the LOP enters the release zone both hands as well as both arms are going to become active. The wrists, particularly the left wrist, is going to start uncocking (ulnar deviation), allowing the clubshaft to drop downward and slightly outward towards the ball. Both forearms are going to start rotating (the left forearm supinating and the right arm pronating) into and through impact. They are not rotating equally; the right forearm is rotating more than the left. If the left arm rotates as much or more than the right it can overclose and deloft the clubface resulting in low traps to the left. In addition it can result in excessive "bowing" of the left wrist that can produce drag which slows down the whipping motion of the club release from the right side of the handle to the left resulting in a loss of distance. As the right forearm is rotating it is also moving outward as noted before, closing the hole between the arms. A further note on this right arm motion and the left wrist unhinging that allows the clubshaft to drop is to link those two motions to a plane. A downswing golf plane is an amalgam of outward and downward elements. In the LOP release the right forearm is pointed somewhat horizontally and rotates outward, fulfilling the outward element while the dropping shaft (unhinging left wrist) supplies the vertical element. In review of this step, for the LOP, from the top of the backswing, the left arm PULLS the club handle downward at the target line. As the LOP enters the release zone, the left wrist starts to uncock, allowing the clubshaft to DROP, and the right arm starts moving OUTWARD as the right fore arm rotates.

If the clubshaft is being pulled by the left arm, dropped by the left wrist and the right forearm rotates in the LOP release, then what is happening in the RIT release? Just about the opposite is what's happening. The left arm with the RIT release is now the passive one.

There is no pull from the top of the backswing with the left arm at the target line whatsoever—period. To pull with the left arm at the ball/target line during the downswing destroys the RIT release. What happens is both arms simply drop (without any pulling of the left arm) from the top of the backswing while the right arm and wrist starts THROWING the shaft outward. The throw is NOT a casting or uncocking of the wrist. That move is called ulnar deviation and is not what we want. What we want is flexion, or throwing motion of the right wrist to begin as soon as you like, to start throwing the shaft outward AS THE ARMS DROP. An important note on the arms in this section as they drop and the right wrist throws is that there is NO COUNTERCLOCKWWISE ROTATION OR PRONATION OF THE RIGHT FOREARM. The first half of the throw must send the shaft outward in the downswing and then the throw's completion will send the shaft upward and left in the follow through. Any counterclockwise rotation of the right forearm as it moves through the impact zone will not allow the shaft to be thrown onto the correct plane. THE RIGHT ARM DOES ROTATE COUNTERCLOCKWISE IN THE FOLLOW THROUGH BUT NOT UNTIL IT HAS EXITED THE RELEASE ZONE. The fact there is no counterclockwise rotation of the right forearm means there is no shaft rotation in the zone for the RIT release. The arm drop and wrist throw is a simultaneous movement of the arms and wrists. They start dropping and throwing at the same time. It's the same motion that long hitting champion Jeff Flagg wrote about when describing the throw as skipping a flat stone across a pond and Ben Hogan wrote about regarding the motion of the right arm being similar to that of an infielder who has fielded the ball and throws to first base, HALF SIDEARM AND HALF

UNDERARM. The drop and throw is exactly that and it happens right from the start. Interestingly a line approximately half sidearm and half underarm is 45 degrees and that's approximately the plane line the RIT is releasing on—more on the plane later.

Ever heard the expression "club stuck behind you"? Well, if in the RIT release you do not throw and drop that's exactly what you will end up with—the club stuck behind you. If you pull your arms out in front of you like an LOP release and are trying an RIT release or your swing plane demands you use an RIT release, you are doomed. You are dead in the water. You have the club stuck behind you and getting your arms more in front of you will only make it worse. You don't need your arms in front of you—you need the club to come back around in front of you. That's why you must THROW the shaft outward while the arms are dropping downward and inward. The net motion is a throwing motion of the right arm, half underarm and half sidearm instead of pulling on the shaft with the left arm. The left arm is dropping downward and inward until it is pointing vertically down, well inside of the target line. At this point the right forearm and wrist, which is throwing the clubshaft outward, is pointing at the target line and therefore is now the plane arm. Let me reiterate what I said earlier, while your right arm is doing this there must be no right forearm rotation or counterclockwise rotation of the club shaft. Now let's understand the arms' INWARD movements and why that has to happen.

There's a radius to a golf swing from about the middle of your sternum to the ball. Looking at address from an overhead view the radius distance is filled by about 1/3 arms and 2/3 clubshaft. We need to come back down to that relationship with the RIT release. If you were to pull with the left arm and keep it pointed at the target line/ball AND THROW the clubshaft with your right wrist the clubhead would miss the ball well beyond (outside) the ball. As you can see, when the left arm swings down pointing at the target line/ball *(FIG. 5.5), the arms are now much farther away from you than they were at address. If the throw gets the clubshaft back out in front of you and the left arm is higher and farther from you than it was at address, then the clubhead is beyond the ball.

What's the solution? When you throw the clubshaft outward you also have to move the arms downward and INWARD, back to where they belong so the throwing RIT release allows you to hit the ball. One further point I want you to notice: the different positions of the right elbow in the two releases. In the LOP release, your arms have been PULLED in front of you and your right elbow is in front of your body. In the RIT release the right elbow is not in front of your body it is on the right side of your body. This is a very key point *(FIG. 5.6). If the right elbow were in front of the body and your body had turned (more on the body motion with the two releases later) you could not correctly execute the RIT release because your arms would be too far in front of your body to allow for the correct "return" of the radius. You would find yourself in trouble with a mixture of a PULLING (LOP) release and a THROWING (RIT) release and that will not work. There simply isn't enough room with your body turning to throw the shaft out and also stick your right elbow and arms out in front of you. It's one or the other. Either pull your arms out in front

***FIG. 5.5**

The RIT radius dictates that the left arm must move downward and inward to accommodate the outward shaft throw.

***FIG. 5.6**

The right elbow in the RIT release is NOT IN FRONT of the body, it is along the right side of the body.

of you and drop the shaft (LOP) or throw the shaft out and around you and get your arms back down and inward to you similar to where they started at address.

In review of this step for the RIT release, your arms drop from the top and the right wrist THROWS the clubshaft outward. As you enter the release zone, the arms, particularly the left arm, moves downward and INWARD back towards its original fairly vertical address position pointing just outside the golfer's toes. <u>The right elbow must remain along the right side of the body as the body turns</u> to allow for the correct radius of the throwing clubshaft. There is no counterclockwise rotation of the right forearm throughout the release motion.

To compare in a general review a downswing plane with both the LOP release and the RIT release: A downswing golf plane is an amalgam or mixing of outward and downward elements. In the LOP release, once you have entered the release zone, the right forearm is pointed somewhat horizontally and rotates outward, fulfilling the outward element while the dropping shaft supplies the vertical element. In the RIT release, once you have entered the release zone, the plane is formed in exactly the opposite way—the outward shaft throw fulfills the horizontal element while the downward and inward left arm supplies the vertical element.

General Overview...Beyond Impact:

The motion from impact through the exit of the release zone in the LOP release has the shaft in line with the right arm, making it the plane arm that is swinging up onto or parallel to the plane line. It's the arm that supplies extension—it's the arm you are extending through the ball. It's the counterclockwise rotation of the right forearm that causes the clubshaft to release from the right side of the handle to the handle's left side through impact. This release is what takes the clubshaft off the left arm and aligns the clubshaft with the right arm *(FIG. 5.7). The right forearm continues rotating until approximately waist high or just beyond in the follow through. The left arm starts to fold as it moves inward after impact. In review for the LOP release, the right arm becomes the plane arm because the counterclockwise rotation of the forearms moves the shaft from right of the club's handle to the handle's left side. The right forearm continues to rotate in a counterclockwise motion.

*FIG. 5.7

In the LOP release from impact to the zone exit, notice how the rolling right arm shuts the clubface to the path/plane.

*FIG. 5.8

In the RIT release from impact to the zone exit, notice the throwing and non-rolling right arm closes the clubface to the target but keeps it square to the path/plane.

In the RIT release, before impact, the throwing (flexion) motion of the right wrist aligned the clubshaft with the right arm, and the downward/inward drop of the left arm allowed the right forearm to point at the target line, making it the plane arm. The motion of the RIT from impact through the exit of the release zone keeps the shaft in line with the right arm, and there is absolutely NO rotation of the right forearm *(FIG. 5.8). The forearms will eventually roll over but not until above waist high. The right arm after impact is throwing the clubshaft up the plane line to the left. The left arm is being shoved even further inward out of the way and starts folding very tight to the body an instant after impact. As the swing continues towards the release zone exit, the left elbow and arm continues to be pushed upward and backward out of the way. At impact both wrists are approximately flat, having reached about the halfway point in the total right wrist flexion movement. The right wrist started in an extension position in the downswing, and the throwing motion as you reached impact has it flexed approximately halfway to where it is now fairly flat, in line with the right forearm. The right elbow is straightening as the right wrist continues its throwing motion to full flexion just after impact while the left wrist reaches full extension at the same time. As a result of this throwing motion, the clubshaft is whipped past the handle and upwards around your body to the left. Again, while this is happening there should be no rotation of the right forearm. In review for the RIT release, the right arm remains the plane arm while the right wrist continues its flexion throw and whips the club past the handle and up the plane to the left. There is very little or no rotation of the club shaft or the right forearm until after waist high in the follow through.

CHAPTER SIX

THE TWO RELEASES &
PLANE, PATH, WIDTH, ANGLE,
CLUBFACE, ROC & SPEED

In this chapter I will continue to build your knowledge base leading up to the releases. To do that I will restate some things covered in earlier chapters so please bear with me. Repetition is a good thing, so reading some very important information again is to your benefit.

Plane

The two releases do not release the club on the same plane. This is a very important factor in determining which release will best suit your swing. In the next chapter I will go over that decision with you. Right now I'm laying the groundwork for your decision. Let's start with the LOP release.

The LOP release stays on the left arm plane virtually until impact. The left arm is pulling the handle and shaft of the club downward and outward, moving along a plane that is considerably more upright than the plane angle the shaft was on at address. In fact it is very close to a plane line that would have been drawn at address from the inside of the ball right up through the top edge of the shoulders *(FIG. 6.1). The left arm as it moves downward and outward along that plane is going to arrive at a spot at impact that is considerably higher and farther from where it started at address. This in turn will have the clubshaft—when the left wrist unhinges and drops the shaft—on a much more upright angle than it was at address. In review, the LOP release moves on a more upright plane than the shaft was at address.

*FIG. 6.1

The left arm in the LOP release is pulling the shaft down on a plane line that is considerably more upright than the shaft was at address.

The RIT release moves on a flatter plane than the LOP release. The plane it moves on is parallel to and then down onto the same plane line that the clubshaft sat on at address. This is considerably different from the LOP. In addition, in the RIT release, the clubshaft is thrown onto the right forearm, which becomes the plane arm when the left arm drops downward and inward until it is pointing well down and inside the target line/ball *(FIG. 6.2). This is so important I'll repeat it: With the right wrist throw, the shaft is lined up with the right forearm; the left arm must move downward and inward, pointing at a spot just beyond the shoe tips so the right forearm can move down a right forearm plane that points at the target line/ball. This plane is fairly identical to the shaft plane at address. In review, the RIT release moves on a flatter plane that is parallel to and then drops onto the same plane line as the shaft plane at address.

Path, Angle and Width

The path of the clubhead when viewed from directly overhead for the LOP release is in-to-in. It is however a gentle arc because the plane is fairly upright. The more upright the plane is the more gentle the path/arc becomes. If the plane angle were perfectly vertical (which it is not in a side-on game) then the path when viewed from above would be a straight line. The angle when the clubhead approaches the ball in an LOP release from the inside is fairly steep and swings on a fairly steep angle back upward and inward after it bottoms out due to the more upright plane. The width of the bottom of the swing is narrower, also due to the more upright plane.

Fig. 6.2

In the RIT release the shaft and right arm are aligned together and at impact have returned to the original address shaft line.

The steeper angles and narrower bottom generally produce higher ball flights because the clubhead's moving down, under and up during impact will spin the ball up the clubface more.

The path of the clubhead for the RIT release as it moves along a plane parallel to and then onto the address shaft plane is decidedly in-to-in. It is a fairly pronounced in-to-in arc because the path/arc when viewed from above on a flatter plane is more circular. The angle when the clubhead approaches the ball from the inside is fairly gentle, sometimes even sweepy, and swings on a shallow angle back upward and inward after it bottoms out, due to the flatter plane. The width of the bottom of the swing is fairly wide, also due to the flatter plane. The shallower angles and wider bottom will generally produce lower ball flights because the hit is more level and less down, under and up, and the ball will resist sliding up the clubface, resulting in the somewhat lower shots.

Clubface and ROC

As mentioned in Chapter One, the clubface as it travels in the downswing and follow through is relative to two distinctly different things: the target and the plane/path. Both releases feature clubfaces that, coming into the release zone, are open to the target. They will be closing during the release and will both exit the release zone closed to the target. Both releases have in common clubfaces that are square to the target for only a short moment. This is pretty much standard for all side-on games where there is a clubface to the respective sport's club, racquet, paddle or stick. In addition to both releases going from open to closed in relation to the target, both releases finish the backswing with clubfaces open to the plane/path. The amount they are open depends on the golfer's grip and left wrist position at the top of backswing. The stronger the left hand is positioned on the grip at address and/or the more "bowed" his left hand position is at the top of backswing the less open to the plane/path he will be *(FIG. 6.3).

Conversely, the weaker the left-hand grip and/or the more "cupped" he is at the top the more open the clubface will be. Regardless of whether it is more or less open to the plane/path, the reason it is open at all is because of the way we cock our hands in the backswing. A "square" clubface to the plane/path throughout the swing would be at a constant 90-degree angle to the plane/path (see *FIG. 4.1, page 39). Keeping it in this position does not allow the golfer to cock his hands in a powerful manner. In fact with a neutral grip, cocking the club while keeping the clubface square to the plane/path results in a powerless collapse of the swing width, plane and arc. In order to powerfully cock the wrists and keep the swing's width, plane and arc, the clubshaft must be rotated, or twisted, clockwise approximately 90 degrees. This open-to-the-plane clubface position at the top of the backswing we actually call "square." It's one of those unexplainable and peculiar things about golf and its language. "Square" at the top is actually 90 degrees open to where it started with a neutral grip at address. To state again, both releases finish the backswing with clubfaces open to the plane/path. So if both releases start the downswing with similar clubfaces and both close relative to the target, what about the clubface is so different between the two releases?

***FIG. 6.3**

Photo 1 shows a square clubface position with a neutral grip and neutral left wrist at the top. Photo 2 is an open clubface position with a neutral grip and a cupped left wrist. Photo 3 illustrates a closed clubface position with a neutral grip and a bowed left wrist. Photo 4 is an open clubface due to an overly weak grip and a neutral wrist at the top. Photo 5 is a closed clubface due to an overly strong grip and a neutral wrist at the top.

What is so different between the LOP release and the RIT release is twofold. First, the RIT release has hardly any shaft rotation to send the clubface closing relative to the target while the LOP has a high degree of shaft rotation to do so. Second, in the RIT release *(FIG. 6.4), the clubface is fairly square to the plane/path for most of the release zone while in the LOP release *(FIG. 6.5), the clubface is not square to the plane/path/arc during most of the release zone. THESE ARE BIG DIFFERENCES. These differences can be difficult to understand why they work the way they do so let's go slowly in explaining them. I'll start with the LOP release and how the clubface actually works. I'll show you how that occurs relative to the target and to the plane/path and the release's ROC. We will then look at the same thing for the RIT release. Afterwards we can understand why the RIT release has hardly any shaft rotation to send the clubface

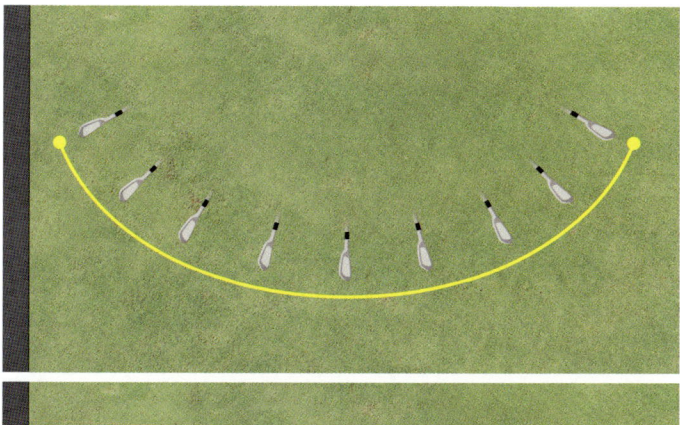

***FIG. 6.4**

The RIT has a slow ROC with the clubface square to the path for a fairly long time.

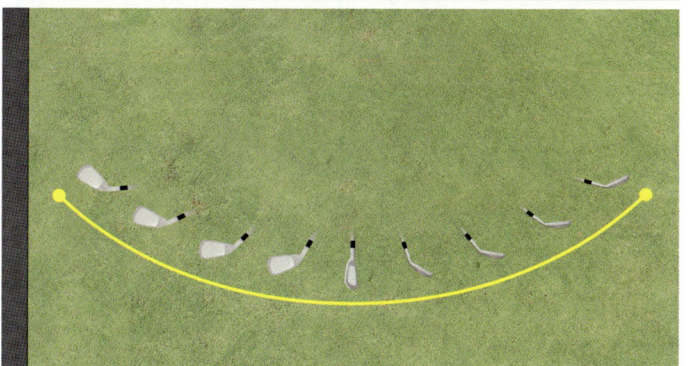

***FIG. 6.5**

The LOP has a high ROC with the clubface moving open to closed to the path quickly.

closing relative to the target, while the LOP has a high degree of shaft rotation to do so. Second we'll understand why, in the RIT release, the clubface is fairly square to the plane/path/arc for most of the release zone while in the LOP release, the clubface is not square to the plane/path/arc during most of the release zone.

The LOP clubface position coming into the release zone is still in exactly the same open position relative to both the target and the plane/path as it was at the top of the backswing. This is because the plane arm at the top of the backswing was the left arm, and the clubface was open to the plane and equally so to the plane arm. Coming into the LOP release zone the plane arm is still the left arm. In fact the left arm has pulled the shaft down and out along the plane. As long as the left arm remains the plane arm the clubface will remain open to the target and to the plane/path until the arms start switching to the right arm as the plane arm just before impact. When the right forearm starts rolling over and shaft rotation begins occurring, several things happen. The clubhead starts moving from the golfer's right side of the handle to the left side, and the clubface starts closing to both the target and the plane/path. As this rotation continues it brings the clubface from open to both the target and the plane/path to closed to both of them very fast. As a result the clubface is actually square to the target and to the plane/path for only a brief moment in the LOP release. Since I have defined (ROC) RATE OF CLOSURE as the clubface closure relative to the path, not to the target, this shaft rotation action would certainly be considered as having a high ROC (rate of closure). The high rate of closure is due partially to the upright nature of the shaft during the release and the length of time the club is held in an open position on the left arm plane. The clubface is open because it is on the left arm plane for a long time and the shaft is upright for the same reason, the left arm is higher and farther from the golfer than it was at address as it moves on its LOP plane. Both factors are due to the same thing—the club is being released with an LOP release; and both factors, the upright shaft and the open clubface, play into the resulting high ROC to the target and to the plane/path/arc for the LOP release.

Let's look at why this happens. First let's examine upright versus flat planes and how their differences can affect the ROC. In a comparison between a totally upright, vertical to the ground, swinging club whose path, when viewed from directly above, would be a straight line and a completely flat, horizontal to the ground, swinging club whose path, when viewed from directly above, would be a circle, if both are open to the target 90 degrees: The upright clubface cannot change that open position as it travels in a straight line path while moving circularly (like a Ferris wheel) on a totally upright plane to the target without shaft rotation *(FIG. 6.6). The totally flat club, however, can close the clubface relative to the target simply because its path, while moving on a horizontal plane (like a merry-go-round), creates a circle

*FIG. 6.6

The upright plane shaft cannot close an open clubface without shaft rotation.

*FIG. 6.7

The flat plane shaft closes the clubface without shaft rotation because it moves on a circle.

when seen from above relative to the target. The path/arc is a perfect circle *(FIG. 6.7) and the clubface while 90 degrees open to the target is actually square to the path/arc and closes to the target because it is moving in a circle relative to the target. The totally upright shaft is moving in a straight line relative to the target and therefore will not close without shaft rotation.

By looking at this comparison we could conclude that the more upright a shaft angle the more shaft rotation is required to close the clubface relative to the target, and the higher ROC the shaft would have. Let's look beyond the high ROC for an upright shaft and study the LOP release itself to see how it could contribute to a high ROC regardless of the shaft angle. That's a very easy one to understand. The LOP release has a very high ROC because the shaft is being swung with the left arm, which results in the clubface being held open for a very long time. Understanding this, we can see that regardless of the plane the shaft is on, the longer the clubface is held open the higher the ROC. In summary, both the upright shaft and the held-open clubface contribute to the high ROC in the LOP release. Undoubtedly the held-open clubface probably is the greater contributor.

The high ROC means there is only a small window of opportunity to hit a straight shot using a LOP release, particularly with a straight faced club. The less lofted, straight faced clubs hit close to the equator of the ball and clubface that is not square to the path will impart maximum side spin to the ball. These are the clubs we hook and slice the most. More lofted clubs hit much lower under the ball's equator resulting in more backspin and much less side spin. Because of this, even with the same degree of open or closed to the path clubface issue, they will hit much straighter shots. Therefore, how does a golfer with an LOP release play consistent repetitive shots with his longer clubs? It simply means the LOP release requires golfers with their straight faced or low lofted clubs to work the ball instead of strictly relying on straight shots. With the clubface so open to the plane/path entering impact and immediately becoming closed to it, the LOP release golfer MUST decide which side of a square clubface he wants to play on. Meaning his go-to shot with straight faced clubs must be primarily a fade or a draw. But please do not let a straight shot hurt you. If there's water down the left side don't aim out into the middle of the lake and play a fade because an accidental straight shot would be wet. In review with some repetition, straight faced clubs like your driver, three wood, three, four and five irons contact close to the side of the ball, near the equator. Any clubface too open or closed to the plane/path will hit wild shots with these clubs because striking the equator or close to it maximizes the amount of sidespin imparted by the open or closed clubface. Conversely, more loft on the clubface means more backspin and less sidespin.

Even with the identical closed or open clubface-to-path relationship, you can't miss a five wood off line as much as a three wood or, worse, a driver. Since the poor clubface to path alignment affects these straight faced clubs the most, choose which way you want to work the ball with them and save the straight shot efforts for the more forgiving lofted clubs. Bubba Watson uses an LOP release and he has it right, he plays big cuts and draws. Jack Nicklaus nearly always played a fade, same with Colin Montgomerie, Mark Calcavecchia, Bruce Lietzke,

K. J. Choi—while Tom Watson, Payne Stewart, Curtis Strange and Cristie Kerr played draws. Phil Mickelson, Bubba Watson, Tiger Woods and others move the ball both ways. Trying to repetitively play straight shots with the straight faced clubs is way too difficult. Bubba once said it so beautifully when asked which hole is the most difficult for him at Augusta National. He replied: "The eighteenth is. I have to hit a straight ball off that tee and I don't play straight balls."

Let's look now at the RIT release and understand why the clubface can go from open to closed relative to the target and stay square to the plane/path without shaft rotation—with a very low ROC. As we laid out earlier, both releases have in common a clubface around 90 degrees open to the plane/path at the top of the backswing and start of the downswing. What happens with the RIT release that gets that clubface in a position where shaft rotation is not a factor in the release? What happens is the clubshaft does not stay aligned with the left arm for a long time. The plane arm starts shifting towards the right arm early in the downswing, so by the time the swing reaches the release zone the switch is underway. This was Hogan's secret and why, as noted previously, he said he hit the ball as hard as he could as soon as he could with his right hand. He felt he couldn't hit it too hard with his right hand and in fact declared he wished he had two right hands. He later went on to proclaim he wished he in fact had three!

The sooner you can align the shaft with the right arm the better in the RIT release. The clubface is open at the top to the LEFT ARM PLANE. As long as it stays on the left arm plane it will remain open to the plane/path. The right arm at the top is just under 90 degrees

***FIG. 6.8**

In Photo 1 note at the top of backswing the plane difference between the left and right arm is approximately 90 degrees and the shaft is aligned with the left arm and the clubface is 90 degrees open to the plane. In Photo 2 the shaft is still aligned with the left arm and the clubface is still 90 degrees open to the plane. In Photo 3 the shaft is aligned with the right arm and the clubface is square to the plane.

to the clubshaft and to the left arm as well *(FIG. 6.8). Because of that nearly 90-degree difference of the right arm to the left arm and the shaft, when the shaft lines up with the right arm it also automatically becomes square to the plane/path. It does not need to be re-rotated back to where it was. If you re-rotated the shaft it would simply make it square to the left arm plane (and 90 degrees closed to the right arm plane) which is exactly what the LOP does at impact. By aligning the clubshaft with the right arm and dropping the left arm downward and inward, the clubface automatically returns to square to the plane/path without rotation *(FIG. 6.9).

Since we have already seen earlier in this chapter that the RIT release is on a flatter plane, now the golfer simply must keep the club moving around on its more circular path to both keep it square to the plane/path and to close the clubface relative to the target without any shaft rotation. That's why there is either very little or no ROC in the RIT

*FIG. 6.9

The shaft is aligned with the right arm and the left arm drops downward and inward to allow the right arm and shaft to perfectly align with the ball at impact.

release. Low ROC means you have a very stable clubface. Your natural shot will be fairly straight balls. They might be slight pushes or pulls but they will fly pretty straight. That does not mean the RIT golfer cannot hit draws and fades if he chooses to do so. He certainly can, and in later chapters I'll show how he can do it and also show the LOP release players how to purposely draw and fade the ball.

In conclusion, the golfer using the LOP release must work the ball, particularly with the straighter faced clubs, in order to be a consistent shotmaker. The RIT golfer is able to hit straight shots because of his stable clubface and can work the ball if he chooses.

Power and Speed

Gaining speed with the release as well as transmitting the already gained speed prior to entering the release zone is done quite differently between the two releases. The LOP release uses leverage plus the rolling of the right forearm to achieve speed, while the RIT uses centripetal force and the resulting centrifugal effect plus the throwing/whipping of the right wrist. Let's first look at the LOP.

Leverage force is an application whereby a force/power is exerted on one end of a lever and an opposite force/power is exerted at the other end. We are going to see that the LOP release uses leverage in two different applications. The first example of leverage is a teeter-totter or seesaw use of leverage where one end is pushed down and the other end is pushed upward. When the seesaw's fulcrum is in the center the forces are equal. The farther the fulcrum is placed from

Fig. 6.10

In the LOP release during impact the entire body is moving upward as a leverage force against the downward moving shaft.

---

the originating force the greater the force will be on the short end of the seesaw. The original force will be multiplied. The opposite is true when the fulcrum is close to the originating force.

In the LOP downswing the left arm is pulling the clubshaft downward from the shoulder. As the swing gets closer to impact, the left shoulder and the left side of the body start rising; and in fact during impact the entire body is moving upward as a leverage force against the downward moving shaft *(FIG. 6.10). This upward motion creates a great deal of leverage power on the downward moving clubshaft and clubhead. The hands act somewhat as the fulcrum of this power and their uncocking adds to the downward speed of the clubhead. Finally, the rolling of the right forearm not only squares the clubhead and closes it as noted earlier, but the rolling motion adds additional power by hurling the clubhead from one side of the handle to the other. This addition of speed is again a result of leverage. A WORD OF CAUTION AS NOTED EARLIER, the forearm rotation must be primarily with the right not the left forearm. If the left forearm over rotates it can result in a shut/delofted clubface and additionally can cause drag, slowing down the whipping release of the clubhead.

A second way to observe leverage besides the teeter-totter illustration is to view opposite forces on the ends of a lever when one end is slowing down and the other end is speeding up. This happens during impact with the LOP release. As the left arm moves slightly inward it also slows down while the right forearm starts rolling outward. The more the left arm abruptly slows down during this right forearm rolling motion, the greater the "shocking" or whipping effect on the clubhead *(FIG. 6.11). It's great if the right arm increases speed as it rolls over and whips through impact, but if the left arm tries to keep its speed up or even increase during impact, the more "drag" is imparted to the clubshaft, robbing the clubhead of the potential whip speed. In fact, trying to increase the speed of the left arm through impact can block the release and, along with the resulting drag, will DECREASE clubhead speed. The left arm must slow down and get out of the way so the outward rolling right arm can both speed up the clubhead and become the plane arm. This slowing down of one element—the handle and left arm—while another element speeds up—the clubhead—is a major feature of the LOP

*FIG. 6.11

The right arm in the LOP release is seen rolling outward and accelerating past the left arm from both down-the-line and face-on views.

release. It is why, when we studied the historical references to the different ways a club is released, one reference was to a leverage motion and another to a hitting motion. Both of these terms refer to the LOP release. They are the opposite of an RIT release, which was historically referred to as a swinging and throwing release.

Speed with the RIT is not achieved through leverage effort. In fact, people who execute the RIT correctly for the first time often comment on how effortless the swing felt. The clubhead's speed is achieved through a swinging/throwing motion, which is the opposite of a leverage motion. A swinging/throwing motion DOES NOT HAVE ONE ELEMENT SLOWING DOWN TO SPEED UP ANOTHER ELEMENT. The RIT release elements, mainly the body, the right arm and the right wrist/club, all reach maximum speed at the same time. Once they start in the downswing they accelerate smoothly and constantly through impact, slowing down in the follow through.

Ernest Jones, in his books about swinging the clubhead, demonstrated this non-leverage swinging motion by using a handkerchief and a pocket knife. With the knife attached to one end of the handkerchief, he would swing the knife back and forth with the hankie, showing all parts of the hankie and the knife reached their respective maximum speeds at the same time. There was no slowing down any part of the handkerchief to speed up the knife—they all swung together.

One thing however is similar between the two releases. Just like speed is generated through two different applications of leverage in the LOP release, speed is generated through two different applications of force in the RIT release.

These two applications that are absolutely essential to a circular swinging motion are centripetal force and centrifugal result. A hammer thrower in track and field certainly creates this motion as does a rodeo cowboy when spinning a lasso around his head. In the RIT, the sooner the golfer can initiate an outward throwing motion of the right wrist the better. This starts the clubshaft moving out from behind the arms in a circular motion. At one and the same time as he throws the clubshaft, he also drops his left arm downward and inward and throws his right arm across his body in a sidearm/underarm motion. When he creates this dropping left arm and circular side arm/underarm motion with his right arm, he creates a centripetal or inward force against the outward circular throw of the clubhead, which in turn starts whipping the outward throw into a circular centrifugal result. The more the right wrist throws/flexion and the closer the right arm throws around and inward close to the body motion, the more it also moves IN FRONT OF the left arm and pins it downward and inward. The left arm is literally being forced into this downward and inward move by the throw of the right wrist and the motion of the right arm. Without this dual action of

***FIG. 6.12**

While the club is moving outward in the RIT release the arms are pulling inward against it creating centripetal force and centrifugal result.

the right wrist and right arm the left arm does not become the inside/pinned arm. As the right arm throws around and the left is pinned down and in, the more this inward force of the arms ties into the body turn and creates tremendous centripetal force. This in turn affects the outward centrifugal circular motion of the club and creates more speed *(FIG. 6.12). The more you can "feel" tight inward arms (I have even referred to the feeling as "little alligator arms") the more you gain a circular whipping club.

Now a HUGE WORD OF CAUTION HERE: Any centripetal/centrifugal motion will fall apart if there is any stopping of the forces. Allow me please to repeat myself here because it is so important: THERE IS NO LEVERAGED STOPPING OR SLOWING DOWN OF THE FORCES IN THE RIT. You must do three things completely and simultaneously. You must 1) throw the right wrist, 2) drop the left arm downward and inward and 3) throw the right forearm half sidearm/half underarm around nonstop. If you stop the right arm motion to throw or whip the clubhead you will fail. You must keep throwing the right arm around to keep the centripetal motion going and you must throw/flex the right wrist to get the clubshaft out from behind the arms and not block the centrifugal result from happening.

In conclusion, the LOP release transmits and adds speed through leverage and the rolling of the forearms, while the RIT release creates centripetal force and centrifugal result through the flexion of the right wrist and an accelerating/non-stop right arm throw in a sidearm/underarm motion that pins the left arm downward and inward.

CHAPTER SEVEN

WHICH RELEASE IS BEST FOR YOUR SWING PLANE?

SEVEN | WHICH RELEASE IS BEST FOR YOUR SWING PLANE?

As mentioned earlier, in my first book, The Plane Truth for Golfers, I wrote that all golf swings, from high handicap golfers to the best players, fall into one of two categories: One Plane or Two Plane. The two categories of swing shape are defined by how you swing your arms and club in relation to your body pivot during the swing. These are categories, not swing models; as I've said all swings, even the worst ones, fall into these categories. If when you turn your body, the arms and club swing AROUND your body while you pivot, you are a One Plane category golfer. If on the other hand your arms and club stay in front of your body and swing more UP AND DOWN than the plane your body pivots on, you are a Two Plane golfer. In other words, either your arms/club swing upward and around you onto approximately the same plane as you turn your body (One Plane) or they don't—period. If they don't, they swing more decidedly vertically than your body turns (Two Plane) *(FIG. 7.1).

These two defined categories of swing shape have been the means of settling most all the conflicting arguments about the golf swing. I heard so many of these conflicting theories while trying to learn the game and on into my playing days that I thought surely all that information couldn't possibly be correct. I've already covered many of the opposites in the release, so you can only imagine how much there is when we talk about the rest of the swing. A sample of the conflicting pieces of advice: move your head behind the ball/keep

*FIG. 7.1

Top swing sequence is an example of a one plane swing where the arms and club swing more around the body and onto somewhat the same plane as the shoulders turn. The bottom swing sequence is a two plane swing example where the arms and club stay in front of the body and swing more upright than the plane of the shoulder turn.

your head still, pull down with your left/throw with your right, stand tall at address/bend over, slide your hips/turn your hips, don't turn your shoulders at the start of the downswing/turn your shoulders at the start of the downswing, keep your arms in front of you/swing your arms around you, stand close to the ball/stand away from the ball, etc. I could keep going but the purpose of this book is not to examine the entire golf swing from address to follow through. It's about the release. I bring these things up only to say I came to find out that all things above are found in correct swings, just not in the same swing. Half of all the above works best in a One Plane swing and the other half in the Two Plane swing. It's also generally true about the two releases; one works generally better in one category than the other. We are going to cover those relationships and also how it works when you mix the categories and releases.

Earlier in Chapter Six we noted the RIT moves on a flatter plane, parallel to and on the address shaft plane line; and the LOP release moves on a more upright plane than the shaft is on at address. The two different swing shape categories also have different planes. The One Plane swing is a flatter swing shape *(FIG. 7.2). It swings up and onto a plane parallel to the shaft at address. In the downswing it swings back down and onto the same plane line as it started on (the shaft line at address). The Two Plane swing is more upright than the shaft plane line at address and is on or slightly under a plane line that runs up from the inside of the ball through the top of the shoulders. Now, it doesn't take a lot to figure out which release most easily fits with which swing type. As a general rule the RIT best fits the One Plane swing and the LOP best fits the Two Plane swing. There are exceptions and we will look at those as well.

***FIG. 7.2**

Top one plane swing sequence swings the shaft upward onto a plane parallel to the original address shaft plane and returns the shaft at impact back to the shaft plane line. Bottom two plane swing sequence swings upward onto a more upright plane drawn from the ball through the top of the shoulders and returns the shaft at impact on or just under that line which is considerably more upright than the shaft line at address.

First, how do you know if you are an upright plane (Two Plane) golfer or a flatter plane (One Plane) player? Hopefully the accompanying photos should help you recognize your swing. Notice I've included the extremes on both categories from the very upright Bubba Watson Two Plane swing to the lower arm Louis Oosthuizen Two Plane swing *(FIG. 7.3). Same with the One Plane slightly higher arm swing of Henrik Stenson and the lower arm Matt Kuchar. Have someone video your swing or watch you and help you decide which one you most closely resemble. Regardless of which category of swing you determine you have, one thing you want is certain: You want to have the clubshaft in the same plane (on plane) as your swing. When the club is off-plane to your swing forces and your swing plane, you will either not hit good shots or the good ones won't be repetitive. Having the clubshaft on plane with your swing is a big step towards good golf. Choosing the release type that allows you to release the clubshaft on plane is critical to your improvement.

If you decide you are a Two Plane golfer then the LOP is generally your release of choice. The exception is the golfer who is a hybrid Two Plane, named that because he has a Two Plane swing but uses an RIT release that is commonly used in a One Plane swing. This golfer would employ an upright backswing, keeping his arms and club in front of him during the backswing while he turns his body.

*FIG. 7.3

From top sequence to bottom sequence they are: low arm one plane swing of Matt Kuchar, slightly more upright one plane swing of Henrik Stenson, low arm two plane swing of Louis Oosthuizen and the higher more upright two plane swing of Bubba Watson.

As this golfer starts his downswing he naturally lays off the clubshaft in the early part of the downswing motion *(FIG. 7.4). Coming down as he enters the release zone, the clubhead is on or close to the shaft plane line (One Plane) while the hands are still in front of him coming down on the shoulder plane line (Two Plane). At this point you could say he has shifted half of the club (the clubhead) onto the One Plane line and the other half is still on the Two Plane line. As he nears impact he goes into a sidearm/underarm throwing motion with his right arm; this causes an abrupt drop of the left arm downward and inward, aligns the shaft with his right arm and also aligns the right forearm onto the shaft plane line. He then finishes with the arms and club swinging around him.

You've seen this golfer and thought he had a very low follow through compared to his backswing. You've also noticed he was an excellent ball hitter when releasing correctly. The Two Plane golfer with the RIT release usually gets there naturally. It's just the way he happened to build his swing. He's a wonderful ball hitter because he has an extremely stable clubface (low ROC) due to the RIT release, with the additional advantage of being able to hit high shots because of his more upright Two Plane position at the top of his backswing. Photos in Chapter Ten show LOP release swings, RIT release swings and hybrid golf swings. Professionals who have Two Plane hybrid swings include Robert Allenby, Inbee Park, Vijay Singh, John Daly, Carl Pettersson and Roberto De Vicenzo, to name a few.

*FIG. 7.4

The two plane hybrid golfers employ two plane upright backswings and then shift to a flatter RIT release around them into the finish.

Examples of this from top to bottom on the following page are Robert Allenby, Inbee Park and Vijay Singh.

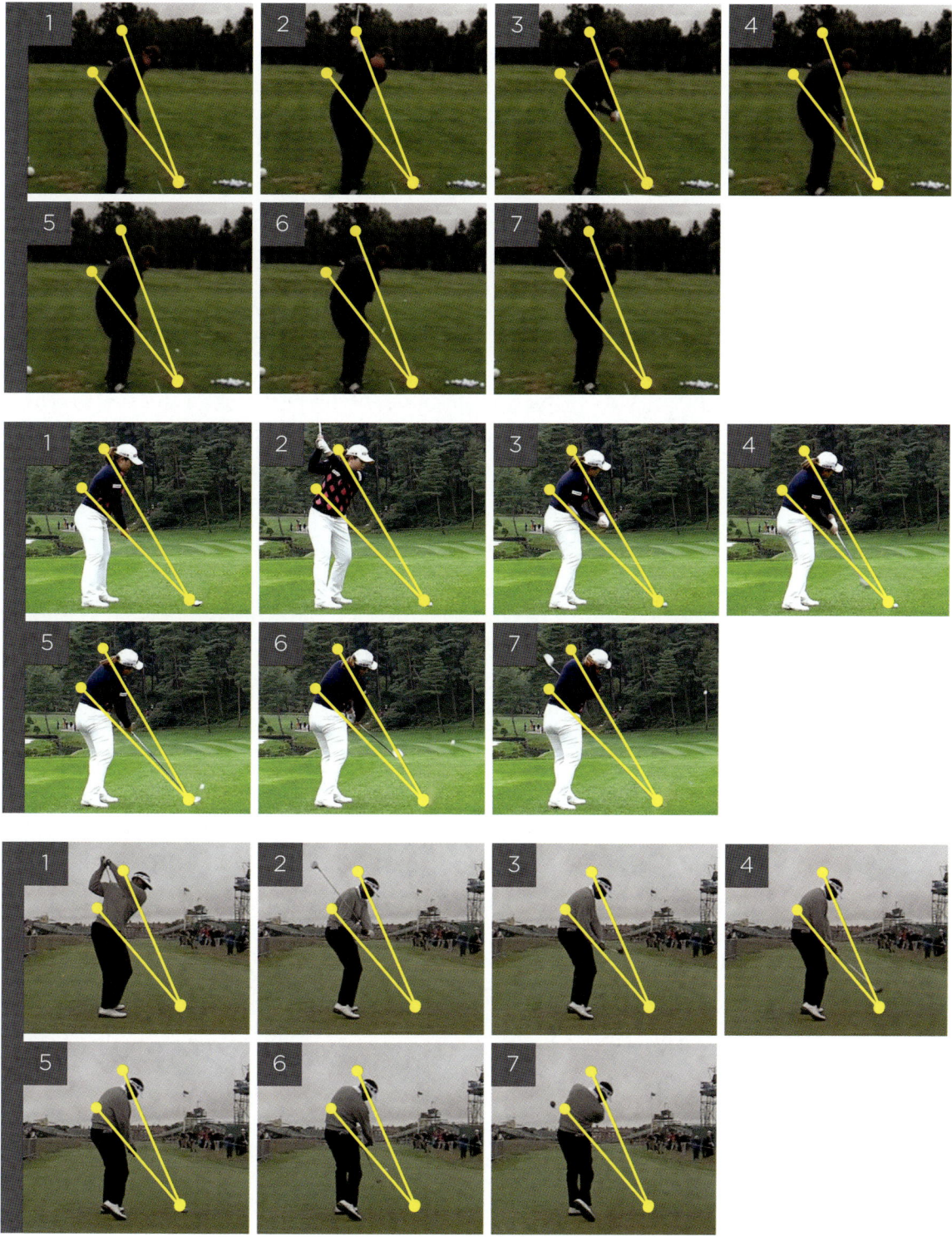

97

Golfers who swing more around with a flatter swing plane are certainly more One Plane and generally use the RIT release. There are some fairly famous hybrid One Planers who use the LOP release but they have to make some modifications to their swings to be successful, otherwise they fail badly. I'll cover those modifications in a moment. The reason the LOP release generally DOES NOT work in a One Plane swing is because the clubshaft in the One Plane swing is being swung in a plane that is much flatter than that of the LOP release. The clubshaft during the LOP release suddenly stands up more vertically and becomes off-plane to the forces of the One Plane swing plane. This sudden vertical LOP shaft position mixed in with a flatter plane swing causes problems. The swing plane forces now affect the shaft by trying to dramatically spin the shaft in a counterclockwise closing motion. It's similar to a rudder broken loose on the back of a boat *(FIG. 7.5); the clubhead flips closed so quickly to the path it's swinging on that disastrous hooks are commonplace. Also please remember the LOP, because the clubface is so open coming into impact and the shaft is somewhat vertical, has a very high ROC. Combine that high ROC with forces trying to spin the clubhead closed and you can understand the dilemma. Because the bad hook is so prevalent, trying to stop the hook by "holding on" or blocking doesn't solve the problem. You are simply trading in a hook for a big push or even a heel shot and shank. Having said all this, the One Planer with an LOP release will hit good shots and play very good rounds followed by disaster.

*FIG. 7.5

The problem for a one plane hybrid using a LOP release is the club shaft comes into impact more upright than the forces of the swing with the clubface very open. As the more horizontal one plane swing forces hit the upright shaft they spin it closing incredibly fast much like a loose rudder on the end of a boat. With the high ROC clubface whirling from open to closed with such uncontrollable speed repetitive shots are almost impossible to achieve.

The problem is the incredible need for perfect timing in order to be repetitive. Without it he hits all the bad shots, with great timing he hits very good ones. This golfer is truly haunted. He going to bed thinking he has it after a good range session only to play the next morning without hitting a good one. The professional golfer with this scenario begins to think the problem is mental because he hits lots of good ones in practice, but is unable to athletically time his faulty mechanics under the gun. The problem is the One Plane swing is coming into impact on a far more rounded inside path than the Two Plane swing. Any fast closing clubface will be closed to the inside path, and a hold-on or blocked clubface will result in a bad push. With the clubhead traveling outward and the more vertical/straighter line LOP release not allowing the clubhead to swing around enough to swing on plane, the clubhead can often continue outward too much and shank the ball. Is there a plane adjustment to the clubshaft an LOP release One Planer can make like the Two Plane hybrid did on the downswing to make his LOP release work? The answer is yes, but let's continue to look at what needs to be solved before we get to the solution.

The problem is the One Plane swing plane is parallel to or on the shaft plane line and the shaft during an LOP release is very upright to that plane. Another way to look at it is the path of the One Plane swing is very rounded and the LOP release is on a much more straight-lined path. Earlier we talked about the term "club stuck behind you." Well here is it again—THIS IS THE CLUB STUCK BEHIND YOU. The clubhead is not coming back AROUND in front of you. THE ARMS ARE COMING BACK AROUND IN FRONT OF YOU

BUT THE CLUBHEAD IS NOT. The One Plane swing with an LOP release is the reason the "club is stuck behind." Even if you tried to throw the club out from behind you, because you have pulled the left arm out in front of you there isn't room for the radius to happen—you would miss entirely beyond the ball. We covered the "club stuck behind you" and the radius issues for a flatter swing plane in Chapter Five. If you need review on this please go back and reread that section. Unfortunately there is no acceptable plane adjustment similar to what the Two Plane hybrid did in the downswing that will allow the One Planer to accommodate the LOP release. The Two Plane hybrid got his shaft flatter and then his swing plane flatter during the downswing to accommodate the RIT release. There is nothing the One Planer can do in the downswing to get the shaft more upright and his swing plane more upright without getting into even deeper trouble. If he attempts to do this he will virtually loop his swing over the top and come into the ball on a steep angle with a vertical shaft.

I've painted a very dark picture for the One Plane swing that doesn't effectively use the RIT release. This was Ben Hogan's dilemma when he was failing for years until he discovered the RIT, and the rest is history. As I mentioned earlier, there is hope for the One Planer who simply cannot properly execute the RIT. To be successful he needs to do a couple of things and then possibly accept a limitation on his power and on the height of his shots. There are numerous golfers in the Hall of Fame who made these adjustments and had great careers. So let's see just what they did that allowed them to be One Plane hybrids using an LOP release.

First off these successful One Plane hybrids played with a closed clubface. They usually employed a strong left-hand grip at address and or had a bowed or closed left-hand position at the top of their backswings (see shut clubface photos *FIG. 6.3, page 70). These "shut" clubface positions were key to their success. As noted earlier in this discussion, the One Planer with an LOP release has a clubshaft and a clubface that rotates shut during impact with incredible speed—like the loose rudder. Well, these successful golfers don't need to let the clubface close. Because of their shut clubface positions they are already fairly square to the path and the plane. During impact they simply don't release. They use every part of the LOP release except the release part *(FIG. 7.6). They don't allow the forearms to rotate and don't allow the clubhead to pass from the right side of the hands to the left side of the hands until well after impact. In other words, they block out the release and drag the clubshaft through impact. Because of this they have a very stable clubface. In fact they are possibly the straightest ball hitters in golf. Unfortunately there are two things they have somewhat given up to gain their great accuracy: speed and height. They tend to be average to below average in length and are often low ball hitters. There is one other factor you will see in most, but not all, of the One Plane hybrids: they aim to the left and swing inside out to the right. This is because the LOP doesn't allow the rounded path coming into the ball to go around an equal amount during and after impact. When they block the clubface they do so while still swinging in-to-out and with their left aim, push the ball onto their target. Examples of famous golfers who are One Plane hybrids are Lee Trevino, Paul Azinger, Fred Funk, Zach Johnson and Jordan Spieth.

*FIG. 7.6

The one plane hybrid uses a shut face with the LOP release and eliminates the very high ROC by blocking the club's release and holding the clubface square to the plane/path.

A note I need to inject at this point concerns this shut face blocking out, which stabilizes the clubface for the One Plane, more rounded golfer who employs the LOP release. Why didn't I recommend the more upright LOP Two Plane golfers also use this shut face blocking to cut down on the LOP's ROC and stabilize their clubface? Instead I told them to "play on one side of the clubface or the other" and purposefully shape their shots. There is a reason and it has to do with earlier discussion we had about the width to the bottom of the swing. Remember the tractor tire illustration? The more upright the swing, the narrower the bottom and conversely the flatter the swing the wider the swing's bottom part during impact. When you employ a shut face blocking motion you have to keep the club's handle well ahead of the clubhead. This fairly extreme forward leaning shaft causes very narrow and steep angles to occur during impact. To apply them to a swing that already tends to be too narrow and steep is a recipe for either a ball flight disaster or a physical disaster. For an upright swing to shallow out a shut face blocking release puts unbelievable strain on the lower back, left shoulder and left hip. With the wider swing bottom of the One Plane swing the strain is far less. The strain is still there for the One Planers as the physical toll shows with such noted players with LOP shut face blocking releases as Lee Trevino and Paul Azinger, who have suffered bad backs. In summary, the solution of shut face blocking to reduce the high ROC of an LOP release works for a One Planer but doesn't work for the more upright Two Plane swing.

Before we move on to the next two chapters I want to cover some things that will greatly help as you get into the actual execution of the releases. Hopefully by now you have an idea of which release you could most easily incorporate into your swing—and I hope you are itching to get on with learning how to execute it. That's what these next two chapters are all about—getting you to correctly release the club through the release zone. The results we're looking for are more predictable shots, with greater consistent power and to accomplish both more repetitively. The release is your key to achieving all these things but it must be done correctly.

The way you're going to accomplish that is through understanding two very different things. The first one is learning exactly what you must do to release the club correctly; what that is verbally, what it looks like and what it feels like. We all learn through these three skills: verbal, visual and kinesthetic. The second objective is to thoroughly learn what your default release is. To put it in less diplomatic terms, the second objective is to be totally aware of your mistake. Understanding these two issues is paramount to learning any skill. One of the two is actually more important than the other. I won't ask you which one is the more important because all of us usually guess the wrong one; so I'll just tell you which one it is. It's the second one—our mistake, our default release.

Surely you are wondering why that is more important than the new stuff. It's more important because no change is accomplished in a blank universe. It's always a move away from an established condition and therefore it has a relationship to what is your natural release. It's learning through comparison, like yin and yang, or salt and pepper. You have to know your starting place backwards and forwards;

verbally, visually and kinesthetically. You cannot change what you do not feel or understand. So understanding your mistake and feeling it is at least as important if not more so as understanding the new moves that you need to make in order to correctly execute the release. These new moves have a certain relationship to your old ones, and in order to understand them and accomplish them you need to understand and feel them in relation to what is normal to your swing. Once you can do that you have the "Ah ha" moment when the lights go on. You can suddenly "see"—this is what I normally do and this is what I want to do—I got it!! That's what we are after.

I designed some drills to additionally aid in your understanding of the two releases, how to execute them, how to use them to shape your shots and how to correct your default mistake. Text in the next two chapters refers to these drills but the details of all the drills are located in Chapter Ten.

To get you to verbally understand the correct release, I'll talk you through exactly what you need to do. I'll visually show you how it looks through photos in the next two chapters as well as photos of correct swings in Chapter Ten. Finally I'll walk you through what the release should feel like to you. To understand your default mistake,

I'll show you photos of the mistakes commonly made along with their resulting ball flights. I'll also talk you through those mistakes so you can identify which one you're making as your default, and I will also show you how to correct it. My hope is you'll eventually feel your default when you don't make the correct release and understand exactly what you need to do to correct it. Until then your ball flight misses will identify your mistake and you'll see the photos of your default and be able to compare them with the correct release.

Before we start allow me to review the six motions of the wrists that I covered in Chapter Five. They were listed in three pairs: Throwing (Flexion and Extension), Twisting or Rotating (Supination and Pronation) and Hinging or Cocking (Ulnar Deviation and Radial Deviation). I'll use both the laymen's terms and the medical terminology in describing how to execute the releases. For further review refer to the chart in Chapter Five on page 49.

CHAPTER EIGHT

EXECUTING THE LOP RELEASE, LOP SHOT SHAPING & LOP MISTAKES

Let's start with what happens in the correct execution of the LOP release. Initially I'm going to cover only what the arms and club motor is doing during the release since that is the engine of the release. After we have thoroughly discussed what the arms and club do during the release I will go through what the body motor does to support the release.

Correct LOP Release | Arms and Club Motor

A great way to visualize the correct LOP release is to imagine an overhead view of dual curving railroad tracks with a switching section incorporated into the curve. There are two train engines moving in the same direction and at the same speed along the curved tracks, one engine on each set of tracks *(FIG. 8.1). The top rail locomotive, the LA (stands for left arm) is slightly ahead of the bottom rail locomotive, the RA (right arm). As the LA nears the ball it starts to slow down dramatically and move off the top rail towards the bottom rail; and immediately thereafter, the bottom engine suddenly starts accelerating and switching upward for the top rail. This locomotive "crossover" illustrates what must happen just prior to and during impact when the left arm (the plane arm) starts dramatically slowing down and moving slightly inward so the right arm can ROLL outward with acceleration and take its place as the plane arm. This crossover along with the rollover of the right arm, when completed, releases the clubhead from the right side of the handle to the left side, rotates the shaft and the clubface from open to closed to both the target and to the path and adds acceleration speed to the clubhead. This is the heart of the LOP and first we need to cover the basics of it.

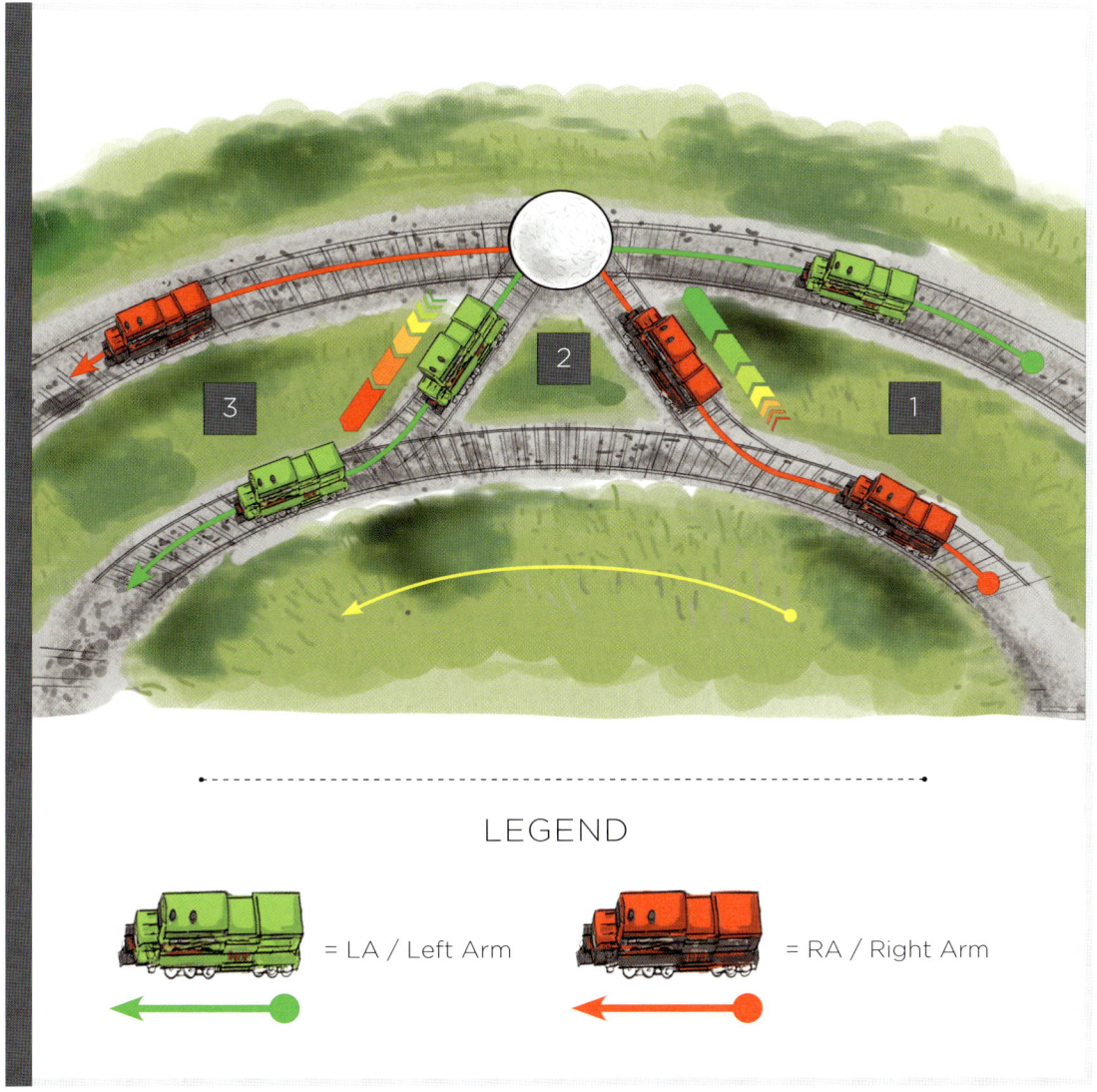

*FIG. 8.1

Coming into impact the left arm, represented by the green train, is the lead train and is lined up with the ball on the outside track. It is the plane arm. Just before impact it starts to slow down and drop towards the inside track and at one and the same time the right arm, represented by the red train, starts accelerating outward towards the outside track. During actual impact both arms are the plane arms for just an instant and then abruptly the left arm continues decelerating as it completes its drop to the inside rail. At this point the accelerating right arm has become the plane arm.

Later in this chapter we'll learn how to shape shots such as punch/low shots as well as draws and fades. But first our objective is getting this release incorporated into your swing so you immediately gain solid hits and more speed.

Let's turn to the photos of the correct LOP release. In these photos look at the top of backswing photo and then the photo as the swing enters the impact zone. There are a number of things I want you to notice: 1) the clubshaft is lined up with the left arm*(FIG. 8.2), 2) the left arm and the clubshaft are either on or UNDER (and fairly parallel to) the address position shoulder plane line to the ball, and 3) the clubface as it enters the release zone is still in the same position as it was at the top, which is open to the plane. These three points are all important aspects of an on-plane LOP position entering the impact zone.

When we view the off-plane positions entering the impact zone we will compare them with these three on-plane elements. The left arm and shaft are on plane to hit the ball at the top of the backswing. They remain on that plane; there is no "plane shift" needed to hit the ball. The left arm has been totally responsible to keep the swing

*FIG. 8.2

Two classic swing sequence examples of the LOP release.

on plane from the top by PULLING the arms and clubshaft mostly downward and somewhat outward without any closing or counterclockwise motion in either arm. In fact if the left arm has any rotation from the top of the backswing to this point it will be to slightly rotate clockwise or open, putting the left arm and clubshaft slightly under but parallel to the shoulder plane line. There is virtually no use of the right arm other than simply to drop with the motion of the left arm. Any closing efforts in getting down to the release zone in either arm will throw the left arm and clubshaft off-plane, as we shall see when we study the LOP mistake photos.

From the entry of the release zone to its midway point, notice in the photos the left arm is still pulling downward and outward at the ball, the left wrist has begun to unhinge and drop the clubshaft and the right arm has started to "wake up." Sequentially the left wrist drop has started just before the right forearm starts to rotate. But it is at this point the right arm has begun to roll and move outward. We can see this by noting the "hole" formed between the two arms has started to close outward and the clubface has begun to close due to the rolling motion of the right forearm.

In the impact photos, we can see the left wrist has fully unhinged. The hole between the arms has pretty much fully closed outward, and both arms are pointing at the ball with the shaft aligned with both arms at this point. If the shaft were more aligned at this point with the right arm you would most probably be playing a draw, and if it were more aligned with the left arm a fade would probably be more the case. The right arm's outward rolling motion has caused the hole to disappear and the clubface to close. It is during this final phase at impact, while the right arm is rolling and moving outward, that the left arm abruptly starts to slow down and move inward. Without this inward slowing down motion you lose the leverage whip needed for power and instead often just block and drag the club through impact. The inward slowdown also slows down the club's handle, allowing the leverage speedup of the clubhead with the right arm and hand.

As we view the post impact photos please note the right arm is now totally the plane arm—it is on the outside set of rails and is rolled over. The right arm is the "extension" arm. The left arm has completed its inward journey to the inner rails. One thing I want you to notice for the correct release: The arms and the clubshaft have already moved back to the inside and are not swinging down the target line. This is proof of the in-to-in nature of the golf swing. If the arms and club were swinging in front of the plane line at this point you would be in-to-out and most likely hitting a hook to the left or a push to the right. If the arms and club were too much left of the target line or under the plane line you would most likely be hitting a pull or a wipe slice. Another thing I want you to notice is the clubface: It is closed to both the target and the path.

In this last set of correct LOP photos the swing has exited the release zone but the positions are still valuable for us to note. The clubshaft and right arm are either on or parallel to the shoulder plane line. The arms and clubface have completely rotated over so the clubface is quite closed to the plane/path.

In review, the following bullet points are essential to a correct LOP release:

LEFT ARM

1) Is plane arm until impact.
2) Pulls arms and shaft downward and outward parallel to or on the shoulder plane line.
3) Clubface remains open until midway in zone.
3) Left wrist unhinges and drops the shaft.
4) Decelerates and drops slightly inward off the plane line.

RIGHT ARM

1) Is passive entering the release zone.
2) Near mid zone it rotates, accelerates and moves outward.
3) Closes the clubface.
4) Whips the clubshaft from the right of the handle to the left.
5) Becomes plane arm at impact to the finish on or parallel to plane line.
6) Continues to rotate to finish.

***FIG. 8.3**

The body motor supports the outward release of the right arm in the LOP release by upward ground forces, a rising spine angle and an outward hip thrust.

(Continued on pg. 117)

Corrrect LOP Release | Body Motor

Let's now review the same photo positions of the arms and club motor we have just studied and look at what the body is doing during these swing phases. Basically the body is in a "supporting" role that allows us to release the club properly *(FIG. 8.3). Some may strongly argue this point and say the body is the lead actor and is not playing a supporting role. I'm not in that camp especially since this book is about the release, which is overwhelmingly controlled by the actions of the arms and club motor. However that does not in any way diminish the role of the body. Its function is to allow, facilitate and amplify the release. One thing is for certain: If the body motor "fights" what you are trying to accomplish in the release it can TOTALLY DESTROY your efforts. So we need to understand just how your body must react to support your release, not destroy it.

At the start of the downswing there has been a lateral slide of the hips with minimal rotation. There has also been minimal rotation of the upper body. As a result of the lateral hip move some weight has shifted onto the left foot. As the LOP release enters the impact zone notice from the down-the-line photo there is a line behind the golfer's hips. That line was drawn at address to show exactly where the hips were when the swing started. Notice how much movement has already occurred away from this address position point. The hips have already started moving outward to support the outward arm release, which in turn has caused the spine to start moving both more upward and upright. These positions are in direct conflict with what a lot of people have claimed are "hallowed" fundamentals of staying in your spine angle. Well, we will see some of those hallowed fundamentals of maintaining the spine angle show up in the RIT release but not in the LOP. There are ground forces that are shallowing out the upright arm and shaft swing by thrusting the hips and allowing the upward body move to supply tremendous downward LEVERAGE forces to the arms and clubshaft from inside of the target line. This is so important! Upward motion supplying downward forces to a clubshaft that is already coming into impact from in front (outside) of the shoulder plane line does no good. The lateral hip slide along

*FIG. 8.4

Note the "stay behind" position that supports the pulling left arm in the LOP release.

with the early hip thrust helps "drop" the arms and clubshaft down on the inside, which is either on or parallel under the shoulder plane line. One last thing to notice is how little the upper body has turned. The lower body has SLIGHTLY turned but has mostly moved laterally. The upper body has held its position.

In the photos from face-on, from the top of backswing into the release zone notice how the left hip has moved laterally back to or even slightly in front of the line it was on at address, transferring weight onto the left foot *(FIG. 8.4). Notice the head has not moved forward from its address position line. Many times it will at this point be to the right of its address position. Also notice as a result of the hip slide and the head line position how the spine is now slightly inclined to the right, away from the target. This is in the "stay behind it" position that you may have heard of before and is important for the LOP release.

As the release moves closer to impact the hip slide has slightly increased and the outward thrusting hip rotation has also increased. Because the head is still steady or even to the right while the hips have completed their lateral movement, the spine tilt to the right has increased.

At impact, the hips have increased their rotation and the left arm has returned to its starting reference line or slightly in front of the original position. The head is at its original start line or still slightly to the right of it. The left side has fully risen and is higher than the right side.

In the follow through all of the weight will move onto the left leg. The upper and lower body will fully rotate and finish standing fairly erect over the left leg. The head will now be closer to the target than its original start line.

In review, the following bullet points are essential to correct body movements in an LOP release:

1) Hips work first in a lateral motion and then turn.
2) Hips thrust and rising spine, supporting the downward pull and the outward arm release from the inside.
3) Upper body delays turning.
4) Spine is slightly tilted to the right and the head is behind the shot.

Correct LOP Release Playing Draws, Fades and Punch Shots

To play shots correctly with the LOP release requires slight modifications to what I have just covered to ensure the ball flight we are trying to play. Remember the LOP release has the clubface square to the path it is moving on for only a brief moment during impact. That moment is way too short a time to predict a straight shot and also be repetitive. That's why all great LOP release players shape their shots, particularly with the straighter faced clubs. They usually have a "go to" shape they prefer, and as you become more proficient with your LOP release you too will find it naturally easier to shape the ball one way or the other. To help you find that way the following will be your guide to shaping your shots.

To play either a draw or a fade you simply need to get the right clubface-to-path relationship. New information has proven the ball starts primarily in the direction the clubface is pointed. So to play a shot that starts in the correct direction, the clubface must be pointed towards your desired start line. The draw has the path more to the right of where the clubface is pointed. Or another way to state the same thing: The clubface needs to be closed to the path you are swinging on. Let's look at this in terms of numbers. If your clubface is 2 degrees open to the target and your path is 5 degrees to the right of the target then the result is a draw *(FIG. 8.5). That draw will hit the target area.

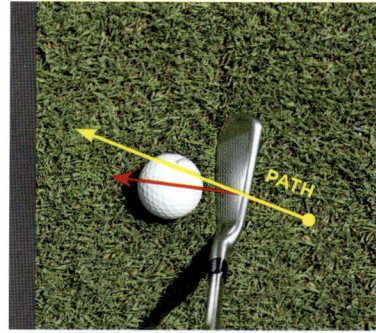

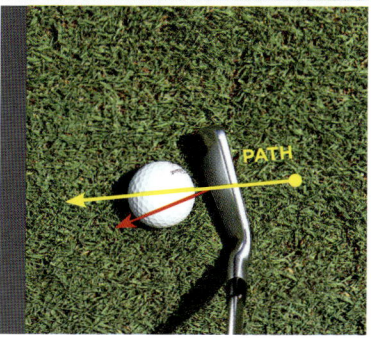

Fig. 8.5

Two different draws. Top photo has the clubface (red arrow) 2 degrees open to the target and path (yellow arrow) 5 degrees to the right. Since the ball starts in the direction of the clubface, this will play a draw that starts just right of the target and curves back to it. Bottom photo has the clubface (red arrow) 5 degrees closed to the target with path (yellow arrow) 2 degrees left. This undesirable draw starts left of the target and moves farther left.

It's also a draw if your clubface is 5 degrees closed and the path is 2 degrees to the left of your target. Unfortunately that draw will be left of the target area. In other words to simply hit a ball that curves left you need to have a clubface closed only to the path it is moving on. To hit a draw onto your target area requires you to start the ball slightly right of the target so when it moves leftward it moves onto the target. To accomplish this you have not only a clubface closed to your path, but also a clubface that is slightly open to the target with the path even more to the right.

To play the draw in relationship to the correct LOP release I've described, first play the ball slightly farther back in your stance than you normally might do. This will place the ball more on the outward/rightward portion of the in-to-in arc, which is where you want to strike the ball for a draw. Earlier than normal in the release you need to unhinge the left wrist allowing the shaft to drop downward a little sooner than usual. Additionally start the right forearm rolling outward sooner and also establish the clubshaft aligned on the right arm plane earlier. In the draw impact photo you can see the right arm and club traveling just slightly in-to-out with the clubface closing *(FIG. 8.6). The handle at impact will be even with or only slightly forward of the ball. If when playing the draw it suddenly becomes too big a hook, simply grip the heel of the right hand firmer against the thumb of the left hand during impact while rolling the right forearm over.

Fig. 8.6

In the draw impact photos the ball will be struck on the outward/rightward portion of the arc with the ball back in the stance. You can also see the right arm and club traveling in-to-out with the clubface closing.

This is shown in the drill photo "Right Hand Pressure" in Chapter Ten. The added grip pressure slows down the shaft rotation just enough for the shot to be a draw and not an out of play hook. The more pressure, the harder you can release and not hook. A full explanation of the "Right Hand Pressure" drill is in Chapter Ten.

In review for the LOP draw shot:

1) Draws have a path/face relationship of face-closed-to-path or path-right-of-face alignment.
2) Play ball slightly back in stance from normal to hit ball on outward/rightward portion of arc.
3) Unhinge left wrist early.
4) Early right arm movement outward; rotation closes clubface and whips shaft past hands onto right arm plane.

The path-to-clubface relationship in a fade is exactly opposite to that of a draw. The fade is produced by a path that is more left of where the clubface is pointed; or another way to say it is the clubface is open to the path *(FIG. 8.7). A clubface that is actually slightly closed to the target can play a fade as long as the path is farther to the left. That particular scenario is what is needed to start your fade slightly left of your target and have the ball curve right onto it. To play a fade, first position the ball slightly more forward in your stance than normal. This will allow you to strike the ball just slightly on the inward/leftward portion of your in-to-in swing. To hit this fade you need to simply delay the timing of the left wrist unhinge drop and

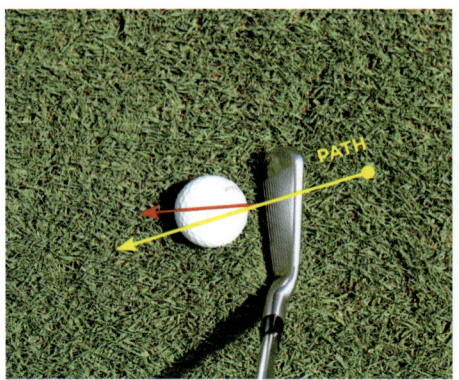 

*FIG. 8.7

Two different fades. Left photo has the clubface (red arrow) 2 degrees closed to the target and path (yellow arrow) about 5 degrees to the left. This will produce a fade that starts just left of the target and curves onto it. The right photo has the clubface (red arrow) 5 degrees open to the target and path (yellow arrow) moving at the target. This will produce an incorrect fade that starts right and goes farther right.

*FIG. 8.8

For a fade the clubhead coming into and through impact is moving inward and leftward with the path left of the clubface.

the right forearm roll and start the inward pull of the left arm slightly earlier. With the drop and the crossover delayed and the left arm coming inward, the clubhead path will slide just slightly across the inside of the ball with a clubface slightly open to the path, making the ball move in a left-to-right fade *(FIG. 8.8). In the fade photo at impact notice the back to the inside path of the arms and clubhead while the clubface has not closed. As a result of this and the forward ball position the club's handle will be farther forward than normal.

In review for the LOP fade shot:

1) Fades have a path/face relationship of face-open-to-path or path-left-of-face alignment.
2) Ball is slightly forward in stance from normal to hit ball on inward/leftward portion of arc.
3) Unhinge left wrist later.
4) Pull left arm inward early.
5) Delay right arm rotation's closing clubface and delay whipping shaft past hands onto right arm plane.

Since a correct LOP release moves along an upright plane it has a fairly narrow, more V type, swing bottom. Because of that down/under/up angled impact area, higher ball flights are fairly normal shots. It's knowing how to play low punch shots that is valuable to the LOP release golfer. To play the punch or knockdown shot you need to take a little part from the fade and three things from the draw. The part from the fade is the forward handle *(FIG. 8.9). The parts you need from the draw are 1) the ball slightly back in your stance, 2) shaft rotation without sending the clubhead forward from the right side of your hands to the left side until AFTER impact, and 3) do not attempt dropping the left arm down early off the upper set of tracks. In fact leave it the plane arm and allow your left wrist to unhinge and the right forearm to rotate to square without the shaft's aligning with the right arm until after impact. Even though the right forearm is rotating, the shot feels a lot like a "block" because you don't allow the clubhead to pass the handle until after the hit. You need to aim slightly left because with the ball back in your stance the inside out path is aimed to the right.

In review for the LOP punch shot:

1) Ball is slightly back in stance from normal with forward shaft lean.
2) Aim slightly left.
3) Unhinge left wrist.
4) Rotate right arm and clubface without allowing the shaft/clubhead to move past handle.
5) Do not pull left arm inward until after impact.
6) Shaft stays on left arm plane.

*FIG. 8.9

The LOP punch shot features a ball back in stance, early shaft drop, right forearm outward rotation and a blocking motion to delay the release of the clubhead past the handle until after impact.

Earlier I talked about the two important issues in improving your swing: understanding the correct move and the mistake as well. We've just covered the correct moves, now your next job is to find your mistake, thoroughly understand it and then compare it to the correct moves. By going back and forth between these two parts of this chapter you will gain the necessary insights to correctly execute your release.

Before we look at the various mistakes that can be made while attempting the LOP release, there's something that can help you identify which mistake you may be making as well as aid in your progress towards a correct release. The use of video is nearly invaluable in accelerating your progress. Incidentally, I ask every Tour professional I instruct to do the same thing. With the advent of smart phones with great video cameras along with a number of downloadable swing analysis apps, you can have your very own video studio in your pocket. When you do take a video, take it from down the line at a point halfway between the golfer's feet and the ball; somewhere near what we refer to as the hand line. Just line up the camera, the hands at address and the target all in a straight line. When viewing the video after importing it into an analyzer, you will draw two different plane lines: one for an LOP release and it will be different for the RIT release which I will cover in the next chapter *(FIG. 8.10). For the LOP release, draw a line up from the heel of the clubhead through the top of the shoulders at address. It should look exactly like the address photo for the LOP release. Now everything you compare will be in relation to that shoulder plane line for the LOP release.

*FIG. 8.10

LOP address with shoulder plane line.

Incorrect LOP Releases: Plane/Path Mistakes and Angle Mistakes

There are two general incorrect releases relative to the plane/path and two incorrect releases relative to the angle.

Plane/Path Mistakes

The two incorrect LOP releases relative to the plane/path are out-to-in and in-to-out. Correct fades and draws are played on in-to-in arcs. The ball is positioned forward or back to change where on the arc you hit the ball, and the clubface is delayed or released early. The two incorrect releases relative to the plane do not have in-to-in arcs.

Out-To-In Mistake

In the incorrect out-to-in release the left arm does not pull the arms and clubshaft enough downward during the early stages of the downswing. Instead the left arm and clubshaft moves outward. In concert with this outward arm and club move, the body is over rotating. The hips have not moved enough laterally to shift weight onto the left foot *(FIG. 8.11). Often the golfer with this release tends to slice his longer clubs and pull the shorter ones. In an effort to stop slicing he tries to close the clubface early by throwing his right arm and hand outward at the start of the downswing. This effort sends the left arm and clubshaft too much outward too soon from the top. He is now in front of the plane. From this start there's not much recovery available to the golfer. If he does manage to get the clubface to close he hits a pull. Otherwise he hits a wipe slice with the clubface very open to his out-to-in path. To correct this release pattern, the left arm has to initiate all movements down to and into the release zone. The right arm and hand must remain passive and not throw outward to close the clubface until just before impact. He must leave the clubface as open to the plane or even more open than it was at the top of the backswing all the way into the release zone. This will allow him to pull the left arm and shaft down onto and even beneath the shoulder plane line *(FIG. 8.12). From here he needs to unhinge the left wrist and release the club as though he's trying to play an intentional draw (see section in this chapter on playing the LOP draw shot).

*FIG. 8.11

LOP out-to-in mistake showing hips backing up and shaft swinging out in front of shoulder plane line to inside and under the line.

*FIG. 8.12

LOP out-to-in mistake correction the clubface is left open as the left arm pulls the shaft down under the shoulder plane line. Then the left wrist unhinges and the right forearm rolls outward to release the club.

In addition to this downward, open clubface entry into the release zone he needs to shift his hips laterally and then thrust his hips right at the start of the downswing in order to support the new motion of the left arm and clubshaft coming into the zone more open and from the inside. So often in golf the initial clubface move in the downswing will reverse itself during impact and it is this very counterintuitiveness that leads golfers to the wrong solution. The out-to-in LOP release golfer is trying to close the clubface early and ends up where it cannot catch up with the leftward path. By reversing that, with the club coming down more from the inside with an open face, it is easy to close the face relative to a path that is more to the right. A drill to help his arm move is the "Bowling" drill. The "Lateral Hip Slide" drill and the "Hip Thrust" drill will help get the body into a better support position. All these drills are detailed in Chapter Ten. Additionally if he tries to hit the draw shot with the rolling right arm release at impact (BUT NOT BEFORE HE GETS INTO THE ZONE) it will help him correct this incorrect release pattern.

In-To-Out Mistake

In the incorrect in-to-out release, the golfer usually fears hitting shots to the left. He may with longer clubs occasionally hit a straight right push, but it's the left balls he fears the most. His mistake is born out of trying to stop the left miss by swinging more to the right *(FIG. 8.13). He's been told he's over the top. That is a terrible misdiagnosis as he is actually too much in-to-out and the clubface is consistently closed to his path, hitting the ball left. This golfer can hit to the left with a clubface that is not closed to the target because his path is so far to the right. His not understanding this is making him try to swing even farther to the right. He needs to try to play fades on purpose (see section in this chapter on playing the LOP fade). He needs to get his left arm to drop down off the upper rail onto the inner rail going left as soon as he enters the release zone *(FIG. 8.14). By bringing the path at impact more to the left and delaying the left wrist unhinge and the right arm rollover he can bring his path around in-to-in. Drills in Chapter Ten that will help him are the "Target Line Stick" drill to get the swing more around to the left and the "Right Hand Pressure" drill to slow down the rotation of the clubface and clubshaft during impact.

*FIG. 8.13

LOP in-to-out mistake showing the left arm and clubshaft coming down too much under the shoulder plane line and then exiting through impact too far in front of the plane line.

*FIG. 8.14

LOP in-to-out mistake correction showing the left arm dropping down and left just before impact and at the same time delaying the left wrist unhinging and the right forearm outward rolling motion.

Angle Mistakes

The two angle mistakes for the LOP release result in the angle of attack being either too steep or too shallow.

Steep Mistake

The LOP steep mistake release has the handle too far forward coming into and through the release zone. As a result the clubhead is trapped too far behind and is still swinging too steeply downward when it hits the ball. The ball flights that result from this miss are usually steep ones like chops and chunks, sky balls or low traps *(FIG. 8.15). Sometimes the golfer with this steep mistake can overcompensate right at impact and abruptly swing the handle straight up to avoid the steep collision and get some opposite results like no divots, heels and even shanks, and straight right pushes. The causes of this steep LOP mistake are: 1) a late unhinging of the left wrist, 2) a non-rotating right arm that keeps the club from being released from the right side of the hands to the left side, and 3) this mistake of the right arm often can be caused by the left arm not decelerating and moving inward—which allows the right arm space to rotate, accelerate and move outward.

To cure this problem the key moves are to abruptly slow down the left arm, unhinge the left wrist and move the left arm inward early in the release zone *(FIG. 8.16). At one and the same time, start rotating and accelerating the right arm outward into the space the left arm has cleared for it. Allow the clubhead to close and whip past the hands. If you should overhook doing this, try the "Right Hand Pressure" drill in Chapter Ten to slow down the clubface rotation.

*FIG. 8.15

The LOP steep impact mistake is caused by starting the unhinging left wrist and the outward rolling of the right arm too late. As a result the handle is too far forward, the clubface is too open and the clubhead is coming into impact on too steep an angle.

*FIG. 8.16

LOP steep impact mistake correction shows a slower moving left arm along with an early left wrist unhinge. In addition the right forearm starts an early outward rotation that allows the clubhead to correctly catch up with the handle.

Shallow Mistake

The shallow LOP release mistake is a throwing motion with the right wrist during impact instead of an outward rolling motion of the right forearm with the clubshaft still on the left arm plane *(FIG. 8.17). This results in an upward scooping motion at impact. This particular mistake is usually with clubs the golfer is trying to hit higher. Because his shots, particularly with low lofted clubs, often don't have enough height, this golfer is trying to help them into the air with a scooping motion. This mistake is also often accompanied by a body mistake of staying on the right foot and not transferring weight onto the left leg. This weight on the back foot helps support the scooping motion. What he isn't doing is transferring his weight to his left leg, unhinging the left wrist and rotating the right arm so the plane arm and the clubshaft gets smoothly transferred onto the right arm plane.

The right wrist in an LOP release works in two ways: It uncocks and twists, BUT DOES NOT THROW. To correct this, the golfer in the impact zone can rotate both arms, not just the right arm. In addition he needs to allow the rotation of the forearms to whip the club past his hands rather than throw the clubhead. Instead of helping the ball into the air with his right palm facing the sky during impact, he needs to feel his right palm on top *(FIG. 8.18), facing more downward as the clubhead whips past his arms. In addition he needs to move his hips more laterally early in his downswing. The "Lateral Hip Slide" drill in Chapter Ten will help. If his divots are deep when doing this, unhinge the left wrist sooner and more completely during the hip slide, just before the forearms rotate.

*FIG. 8.17

LOP shallow impact mistake is caused by trying to help the ball into the air by lofting it with a scooping motion. The mistake made is a throw by the right wrist just prior to impact which breaks down and scoops the left wrist resulting in an upward hit.

*FIG. 8.18

LOP shallow impact mistake correction shows the golfer moving more laterally onto his left leg. There is NO throwing motion and in its place both the right and the left forearms rotate to release the clubhead past the handle.

CHAPTER NINE

EXECUTING THE RIT RELEASE, RIT SHOT SHAPING & RIT MISTAKES

Let's start with what happens in the correct execution of the RIT release. I'll initially cover only what the arms and club motor is doing during the release since that is the engine of the release. After we have thoroughly discussed what the arms and club do during the release I will go through what the body motor does to support the release.

Correct RIT Release | Arms and Club Motor

Several points are vital to your success in both understanding and executing the RIT release. To make sure these points are hammered home I will be using an old tool, repetition, to get my points across. I tell all my students, "I may bore you to death but I don't ever want you confused." So bear with me when I repeat certain topics.

1. To begin instructing you in the execution of the RIT release, I'd first like to give you a visual in general terms of what it looks like using just one arm—the right arm. Grip the club at address, then take off the left hand and raise your right arm and shaft level to the ground, pointing straight out in front of you *(FIG. 9.1). Using ONLY wrist extension, move the shaft level to the ground as far as you can to the right of your arm. I don't want your arm to move; only the shaft and your right wrist. Your arm should still be pointing straight out away from you and level to the ground. Now, using wrist flexion ONLY, throw the shaft to the left of your arm as far as you can, leaving the right arm still straight in front of you. One strong warning while doing this; DO NOT ALLOW YOUR ARM, THE SHAFT OR THE CLUBFACE TO ROTATE OVER!!! I want the toe of the club pointing

upward during the entire throw; do not allow it to roll over. Now, I want you to repeat this exercise several times. Each time you do, I want you to notice several things: 1) the shaft is aligned (is in a perfect extension—the shaft and right arm are both on a plane parallel to the ground) with the right arm, 2) the clubface constantly closes relative to the target but is always square to its path as you flex/throw the wrist WITHOUT ANY ROTATION, 3) the clubhead goes in a perfect in-to-in arc and 4) the loft on the clubface stays constant. These last two points are important to your understanding of why the RIT hits straight shots and produces consistent, predictable distance control particularly with the short irons. The square clubface to the path equals straight shots. The constant loft through impact results in repetitive distance control for short irons. Hitting the ball to a predictable yardage is the secret to success in the scoring zone between 150 and 100 yards from the green. With an understanding of these four points and if I said nothing else you now have a perfect picture of a totally stable closing clubface on an arc—a face that is always square to the path it is traveling on and possesses the constant loft necessary for predictable short irons.

***FIG. 9.1**

One hand throwing drill level to the ground with NO rollover.

2. Now let's change this visual exercise a little. I want you to go again to the start position out in front of you level to the ground. From here simply drop the right forearm down halfway to the ground *(FIG. 9.2). It should be now on a 45-degree plane which is approximately the same as the shaft plane at address. Now repeat the right wrist extension and flexion, holding your arm steady in place, pointing at the ground at a 45-degree angle (same motion as when your arm was parallel to the ground); again WITHOUT ANY ARM ROTATION. Notice how now in the forward swing the clubface is constantly closing to the target but is square to a shaft plane while moving on an arc downward and outward and then back upward and inward. This illustration is invaluable to your understanding of the RIT release.

Before we move on to a step by step analysis of the RIT release I want you to be particular about your right-hand grip. I want you to examine your grip in two distinct ways. It must be in the fingers and must be positioned on top of the left hand, not underneath the club *(FIG. 9.3). These are vital points in your success with the RIT release. Now hold the club as I'm showing in the RIGHT-HAND GRIP photo. Your grip in the right hand should NEVER BE IN THE PALM—only in the fingers. Everything else should be off and not touching the club. Next I want you to check the second photo, RIGHT HAND ON TOP. This is also a very important element of the RIT release. If your right-hand grip is too far underneath, the throw will not square the clubface and will additionally throw the shaft off plane.

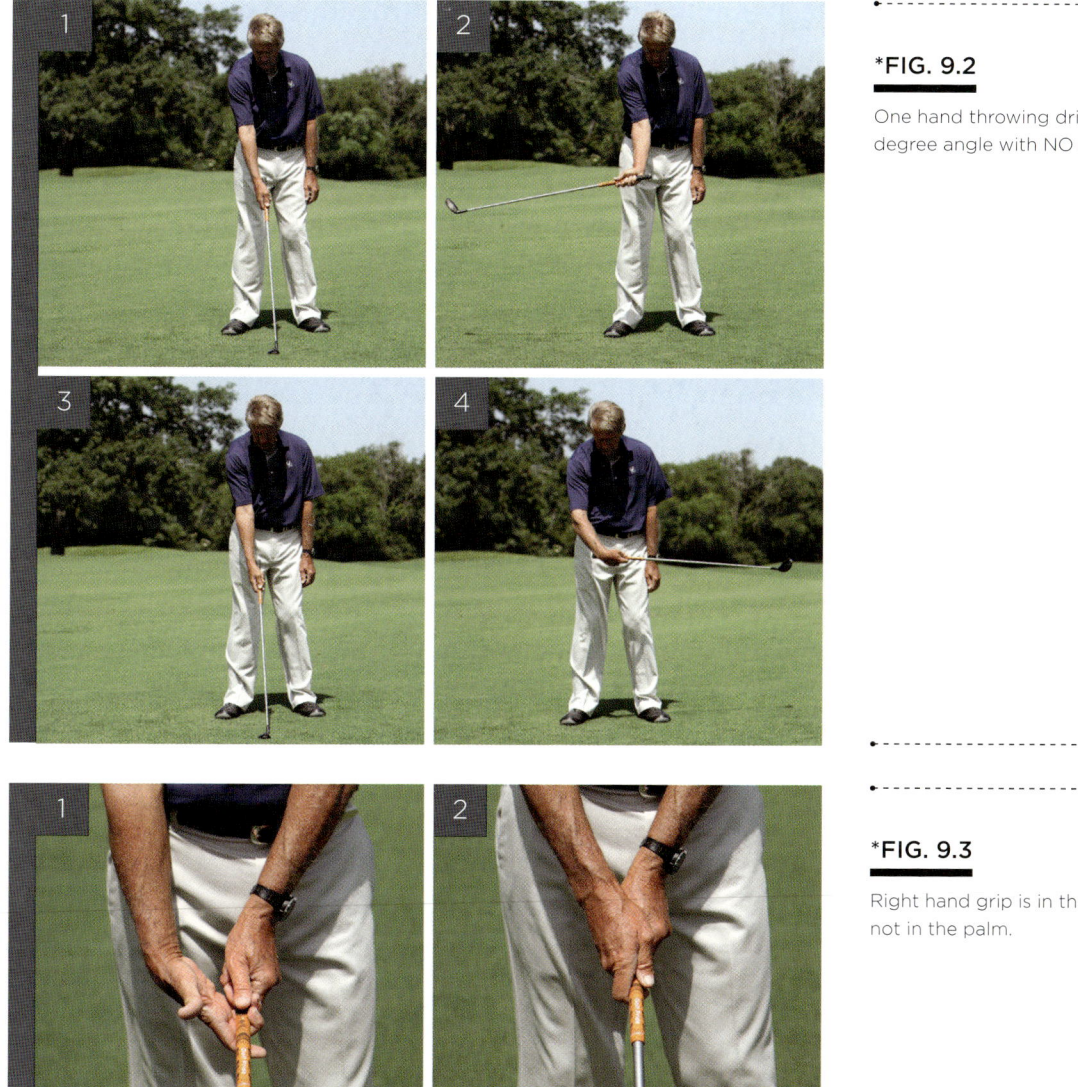

*FIG. 9.2

One hand throwing drill on 45 degree angle with NO rollover.

*FIG. 9.3

Right hand grip is in the fingers not in the palm.

Now we're going to repeat the above shaft plane exercise, making sure you're holding the club in only the fingers of your right hand. Again, do not allow the wrist, arm or shaft to rotate over. I'm hoping as you do it over and over again you will feel a number of things. First I want you to feel the huge difference between leverage effort and effortless swinging or throwing. Holding the club more in the palm feels like you have more control and strength. In the fingers it feels a little out of control. That's what I want. I don't want too much club control or too much tension in the right hand; I want quickness and speed. The left hand has control and strength because we hold it across the palm. The right-hand throw must be quick. Fast balls are thrown off the fingertips not out of the palm. We have no power in our fingers but we have speed. We have light, easy, effortless speed. It's the difference between a gazelle and a rhino; one's pure speed and the other is pure power. In the RIT we are trying to stay away from leverage and power as far as we can. We want speed, we want a swinging motion, we want to throw one hundred-plus mph fastballs. Like a "rag-arm" pitcher whose arm is loose to the point of being limp, the RIT golfer needs to throw with loose joints and limp muscles to the point of "feeling" out of control to gain both speed and control. Once again, YOU MUST GIVE UP CONTROL TO GAIN CONTROL...YOU MUST GIVE UP STRENGTH TO GAIN SPEED.

Now back to a learning exercise. Holding the club again in just your right hand, allow your right arm to swing back just above waist high and swing through to waist high while at the same time throwing/flexing your right wrist. You must do both things NON STOP and without rolling the forearm or clubface over *(FIG. 9.4). It is critical

***FIG. 9.4**

One hand waist high to waist high arm swing with throwing motion and NO rollover.

that you learn to throw/flex the right wrist without any slowdown or stopping of your right arm. The RIT is a swinging motion, not a leverage motion. As such the arm swing and the club swing (club throw) must both be moving, not one (the arm) slowing down while you try to speed the other up.

After you are comfortable doing this, pick a target on the ground like a tee or twig and orient your one-arm swing and throwing motion at the object, trying to hit it. At first you will fail and will try to overcontrol the motion to hit the twig. That's precisely the wrong thing to do. Loosen up and become freer with the swing and throw. As you become less controlling you will actually find it easier to hit the twig. Each time you do this check that you haven't allowed the arm/clubface to roll over. After a while I want you to try making contact with a ball. I'm not looking for a good shot—just contact.

If the ball only rolls along the ground that's fine. Again (repetition here so it must be important) check that the right forearm has not rotated over. You see there are two ways the clubshaft can move from one side of the handle to the other: 1) by flexion and 2) by rolling over. Rolling over is what happens in the LOP. If it happens in the RIT the ROC is uncontrollable. Practice letting wrist flexion release the shaft from behind the right arm to past it while moving the right arm—instead of using arm rotation to move the shaft past the arm. Check your clubface at the finish and make sure it looks like the correct photo, not the rolled over incorrect photo *(FIG. 9.5).

4. Now we are going to do this same exercise with both hands on the club. Little arm swings from waist high to waist high while throwing the club with the right wrist. The major difference you are now going to feel is the left arm is in the way; before it wasn't in the way. We will be trying to "feel" several things in the mini full swing, but we are going to feel them one at a time. First I want you to feel the right wrist throw. This aligns the clubshaft with the right forearm. Then feel the left arm dropping downward and inward until it is vertical and out of the way. This allows the right forearm to be pointed at the target line and become the plane arm. As the plane arm it is now the "outside" or nearest to the target line arm. These moves MUST BE MADE JUST PRIOR TO IMPACT in the area of the release zone midway between entering the zone and impact.

The purpose of feeling these things is to firmly identify two things: one is the shaft alignment with the right forearm, the second is how the right forearm becomes the plane arm. These are two different

*FIG. 9.5

The left one hand drill photo shows a correct, non-rolled over clubface. The photo on the right shows an incorrect rolled over clubface.

*FIG. 9.6

The left photo shows a correct throw aimed above and beyond the ball. The right photo shows while throwing with your right wrist, your left arm, which has been pointed at the target line, has to drop down and into you to hit the ball..

purposes and you must accomplish both to be successful. A second purpose of this drill is to feel how to create centrifugal motion and centripetal force on the club. The wrist throw/flexion starts the motion by creating an outward (centrifugal) force on the clubhead. In fact I want the throw to be so much that the clubhead isn't headed towards the ball at all. I want it headed above and beyond the ball. See the photo with the clubhead above and beyond the ball *(FIG. 9.6). What I'm trying to create is a reason for you to have to bring your arms down and in. By throwing the clubhead on a plane that is above and beyond the ball your arms have to come down and in so you can hit the ball instead of miss it. This down and inward move of the arms and handle of the club creates centripetal (inward) force against the outward (centrifugal) throw *(FIG. 9.7). Now the club is whipping on a tight circle around you. Make practice swings at a twig/tee feeling the outward throw and the tight inward arms.

In review, the tight inward arms were accomplished by the downward and inward dropping of the left arm and the half sidearm/half underarm throw of the right arm across your body. Again, do not allow the right forearm to roll over, and check the clubface at the end of your waist high swings to make sure there hasn't been any rollover. After successful practice swings try hitting shots with this same approximate waist high to waist high swing; trying to exactly repeat the outward throwing and the downward/inward arm/handle motions. Again be careful not to roll over the right forearm. I want your right wrist still in the flexion position and your left wrist still in an extension position at the end of this short abbreviated drill swing. In fact I want it to look exactly like the photo of Ben Hogan at the

*FIG. 9.7

This is the same illustration as FIG. 9.6 showing how the left arm has to drop down from pointing at the target line to pointing at your shoes so the right forearm and shaft now point at the target line/ball.

*FIG. 9.8

This photo shows Ben Hogan in a just above waist high-finish with his right wrist still in full flexion with no rollover. Note the back of his right hand facing the target.

Fig. 9.9

The top of backswing position with the left arm and club for the RIT release is not pointed at the ball. It is on a plane roughly parallel to the shaft plane line.

end of the same swing drill *(FIG. 9.8). This drill is named the "Throw and Drop" and is detailed in Chapter Ten. I recommend you study the drill to further understand how to properly execute it.

This exercise is so important simply because it is exactly the RIT release through the release zone. You can't practice it enough. I'd be remiss however if I just left you at this point and said, "Good job, that's all there is to it." It is all there is to it if you can get from the top of the backswing to the release zone successfully. You know what to do from there. But let's spend a little time looking at what happens from the top to the zone.

First let's look at the photo of the RIT player at the top of the backswing. Notice the plane of his left arm and clubshaft is not on plane with the ball *(FIG. 9.9). In other words, unlike the LOP release position at the top, which is on plane to hit the ball, the RIT at the top of the backswing is on a plane that WILL MISS THE BALL COMPLETELY. It is on a plane roughly parallel to the shaft plane that was established at address. You do not pull downward and outward at the ball to fix this problem of not being on plane to hit the ball. Instead you must undergo a "plane shift" or plane drop onto the shaft plane.

The forces in the RIT release swing are lined up parallel to or on the shaft plane line and MUST REMAIN that way. From the top of the backswing there should be ABSOLUTELY NO LEFT ARM PULLING. The entire downswing to the zone and through the zone must be dominated by the actions of the right arm and the downward and inward dropping of the left arm. The left arm use is limited to only one issue: to drop downward and inward out of the way so the right arm can become the plane arm. The left arm's the plane arm starting the downswing and must relinquish that role as soon as it can. Any other use of it can only interfere with the RIT release.

*FIG. 9.10

As the downswing progresses it is vital that the right elbow hold tight to your right side at approximately the seam of the shirt and not move in front of the body.

The right arm has two duties it must fulfill: to throw the shaft onto the right forearm and to become the plane arm. The right arm is looking to become the downswing hero. As Hogan claimed, he wished he had three right hands/arms. The actual motion with the right arm from the top to the zone is coordinated with a turning motion of the body. If the body thrusts you cannot correctly execute the RIT. More on this later. But as the body turns, the right forearm drops downward and only very slightly outward towards the shaft plane line. Be careful NOT TO ALLOW THE RIGHT ELBOW TO LEAD IN FRONT OF YOU. This is very important because if it does you cannot set up the correct spacing for the radius of the RIT release. We covered this in earlier chapters and I suggest you review the material if you need to refresh your memory.

The right elbow should stay back somewhat aligned with the seam in a shirt running down from the armpit to the waist *(FIG. 9.10). Keeping it there while you swing the forearm down and just barely out towards or even onto the shaft plane line allows the room for the throwing centrifugal and inward centripetal motions to occur. The elbow will move forward away from the shirt seam right at impact and just after as the right arm extends as the plane arm into the follow through. However, during the initial stages of the throw and drop the right elbow stays even with the shirt seam to allow for the proper RIT radius. Again, the left arm must drop downward and inward to vertical while the right arm is carrying out the above motions.

Now that the swing is entering the release zone notice in the photos the turning of the body, the downward/inward drop of the left arm and the down and slightly outward drop of the right forearm have done their respective jobs so the club is parallel to or on the shaft plane line. From here to past impact you do not change your efforts in any way from what you did in the earlier waist high to waist high drill; keep throwing/flexing the right wrist while getting the left arm down and swinging the right forearm and handle inward in a half sidearm/half underarm motion. The left arm is going to be pinned as the inside arm because of the right wrist throw, the left arm drop and the swinging across the body of the right forearm.

In review again, just after entering the release zone you can notice in the photos how the left arm drops downward and inward until it is vertical, pointing straight down. At that point the right forearm is pointed at the ball. Also note while the left arm drops downward and inward the clubshaft keeps moving outward *(FIG. 9.11). The combination of the two motions results in forming a plane pointed at the ball and on the shaft plane line.

*FIG. 9.11

Note the left arm dropping down and inward until vertical allowing the right forearm and clubshaft to point at the ball.

Before going further I want to review some and expand a little on the right wrist throwing motion and exactly what it does. Even though the throw is one CONTINUOUS motion, the throw actually can be best understood by dividing it in two halves. The first half is from when you initiate the throw before entering the release zone to around impact. That throwing of the right wrist does several things: 1) it sends the club outward from behind the right arm and body (remember the part earlier about the "club stuck behind you"); 2) it puts the clubshaft onto or "aligned with" the right arm plane; 3) it squares the clubface with the plane/path and 4) it starts the clubhead on an outward circular orbit.

About the only thing the throw/flexion didn't accomplish was to make the right forearm the plane arm. That happens when the left arm completes its drop to vertical so the right forearm is pointed at the target line. The second part of the throw also does several things: 1) it adds and releases speed as it sends the clubhead whipping past the handle; 2) it swings the clubhead immediately inward off the target line; 3) it closes the clubface to the target but keeps it square to the path/plane and 4) it makes the clubhead move in a circular path

*FIG. 9.12

As the right wrist continues in flexion the clubhead moves on an arc around the golfer. The clubface closes to the target but stays square to the arc.

around and upward on the shaft plane to the left. To allow the right wrist to FULLY finish its flexion, the left wrist has to break down and the left arm to fold as the right wrist throws and the arms move INWARD, around, leftward and upward *(FIG. 9.13). All these things in the RIT release can be seen in *(FIG. 9.12 & FIG. 9.13).

*FIG. 9.13

The left arm and wrist must break down through impact to allow the right wrist to reach full flexion. Note the lack of any roll-over of the right forearm

Allow me to go over this part again. During this second phase, from impact to the finish you just keep throwing/flexing the right wrist. This motion will cause the left wrist to go into extension (fold backward) through impact. Do not fight this!! It must happen in a swinging motion. You may have heard this extension or breaking down of the left wrist is wrong. That may be true for an LOP release but it simply is not true for the RIT release *(FIG. 9.14). You will be surprised as you view the accompanying photos of great players throwing the club through impact. The speed and accuracy produced by this throwing/whipping is tremendous. I cannot overstate this. This is the SECRET of the RIT release. It produces both power and accuracy. The power is obvious. The completion of the throw is translated into whipping the centripetal force and centrifugal result into great speed. This is not leverage, it is speed, and without allowing the left wrist to breakdown/extension with the full flexion/throw of the right wrist simply "checks" this speed like someone check swinging a baseball bat at a pitch he doesn't like.

FIG. 9.14

Excellent view of the left wrist going into extension as the right wrist fully throws.

In the LOP release the completion of the rollover of the forearms during impact whips the clubhead past the hands. In the RIT release it's the extension of the left wrist and the FULL flexion of the right wrist that whips the club by allowing the centripetal and centrifugal motions to continue through the zone. Without it you either check the speed or you roll over and hit terrible hooks. The throw must complete itself through the impact zone without any rollover. The rollover occurs after waist high in the follow through. If it happens earlier then you affect both the completion and the accuracy of the release. The throw keeps the club moving around and square to that path. If you interrupt that throw with a rollover you lose BOTH the arc and the square clubface to the arc. If you roll over you automatically stop the throw which stops the clubhead moving on an arc. Instead of continuing its swing on an arc the clubhead moves on a straighter line. At the same time the clubface ABRUPTLY closes to that straight line with resulting wild shots left.

Bad hooks are not caused solely by the clubface closing. They are caused because as the clubface is closing it is not going around to the left; it is going in too straight a line. If it were going left as it closed the face would be square to the path. With the clubface closing to a straight-line path, the ball goes wildly left. This is a hard concept for golfers to get their heads around but it is the same issue the slicer faces, just in reverse. The slice is a result of the path going left faster than the clubface closes. The hook is a result of the clubface closing faster than the path goes left. It's correct but tough to believe, the hooker (who is already afraid of left) needs to get the clubhead going around to the left more and the slicer (who is afraid of the right) needs to get the path more to the right. It's a game of opposites.

I know I'll sound like a broken record but I'm going to repeat myself again. That's how important all this about the second half of the release is and how groundbreaking this information will be to so many of you. Everything I've presented in this chapter is designed to get you to fully release the club so it moves in-to-in on the right arm plane. The drills I've covered with you along with those detailed in Chapter Ten will help you with this very segment of the release. The "Three Finger Throw" drill is referred to in several of the RIT mistakes and am also recommending it to everyone as indispensable to learning the second half of the RIT release. It's in this second half, while the throw is completing and the shaft is whipping around to the left, the force of this motion breaks down the left arm and shoves it upward and leftward out of the way. Again like the breaking down of the left wrist, DO NOT fight this. The club MUST be allowed to come around to the left. The left arm hasn't been the plane arm in the RIT release for some time now since it dropped downward and inward to vertical, allowing the right forearm to become the plane arm. At this point it can only get back in the way of the releasing power of the entire right wrist, arm and right side as it comes hurtling through.

I'm reluctant to give this advice but even if you have to "feel" as though you pull the left elbow up and back to get it to fold like Lee Westwood does, do it *(FIG. 9.15). If the sidearm/underarm swing of the right forearm across the torso isn't truly pinning the left arm as the inside arm then yank it out of the way. You are not extending the left arm through impact to the finish in the RIT release. It's the right arm that's extending through and you needto get the left out of the way.

In the correct RIT release zone exit, notice how the clubshaft now shows up around to the left of your body either on or parallel to the shaft plane line *(FIG. 9.16). Also notice how the clubface has not yet been closed to the shaft plane line. These two positions are key positions and are very important to the correct RIT release.

*FIG. 9.15

If you're having trouble getting your left arm pinned then yank it upward and inward behind you and force it to fold.

  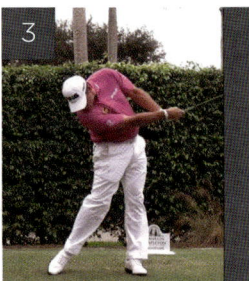

*FIG. 9.16

The throw with no rollover coupled with the left arm drop allows the shaft to whip around the body on or parallel to the shaft plane line.

There are a couple of final points I want to clear up regarding the correct right wrist throw. Those points concern the difference between casting and throwing and the difference between scooping and throwing. First let's deal with the cast versus the throw. The cast is an uncocking (ulnar deviation) motion of the wrists at the start of the downswing. Believe it or not a cast is perfectly acceptable in an LOP release. In fact you must unhinge or cast prior to impact with the LOP. Not so with the RIT. Any unhinging/uncocking (ulnar deviation) should be minimal if at all in the RIT. Secondly let's discuss the difference between a scoop and a throw. Both of these are done with the same wrist action; flexion. The difference is the flexion in the throw is initiated BEFORE the clubhead drops below the line of the right forearm. The flexion in the scoop is initiated AFTER the clubhead drops below an extended line of the right forearm *(FIG. 9.17). This extended line of the right forearm I call the NO FLY ZONE. You must begin the throw before the clubhead gets below this line in order for the clubshaft to align with the right forearm *(FIG. 9.18). If you wait too long and the clubhead drops below the no fly zone, then any throw you will make will still have the clubshaft aligned with the left arm and will be a weak scoop. A correct throw of the shaft onto the right forearm results in a flatter plane and a club that moves on an arc with the face square to the path and the clubface's loft constant as it moves around. A late throw after the clubhead drops below the no fly zone results in an upright plane and a scoop where the clubhead moves on a straight line with increasing loft. This lofting, straight line clubhead produces high and very weak shots. The "Throw and Drop" drill is vital to your understanding of how to correct a scooping mistake.

***FIG. 9.17**

The large photo shows the clubhead has dropped below the extended line of the right forearm and is now in the no-fly zone. Any throw initiated from here will result in a scoop which does not close the clubface and moves the clubhead in a straight line gaining loft.

***FIG. 9.18**

The RIT throw must begin before the clubhead drops below the extended line of the right forearm. The large photo shows the limit of where the throw must have been initiated. If executed properly the throw closes the clubhead in an arc and the loft remains constant.

In review the following points are essential to a correct RIT release:

1) There is no pulling with the left arm during the downswing portion; it simply drops downward and inward until vertical to the ground.
2) The right forearm arm drops downward and slightly outward towards the shaft plane line to get to the release zone while keeping the right elbow along the right side of the body, NOT IN FRONT of it.
3) The right wrist begins throwing/flexion prior to the release zone, and prior to the clubhead dropping below the no fly zone, creating outward centrifugal motion. The left arm's continuing movement downward and inward while the right forearm swings half sidearm/half underarm across the torso creates centripetal inward force.
4) There is NO rotation of the right forearm or the clubhead through the impact zone.
5) During and just after impact the left wrist goes into extension, allowing the right wrist to complete its throw/flexion as the right forearm comes around very close to the body.
6) The left arm folds and gets pushed out of the way; inward, around, upward and leftward.

Correct RIT Release | Body Motor

Let's now review the same photo positions of the arms and club motor we have just studied and look at what the body is doing during these swing phases. Basically the body is moving in a "supporting" role that allows us to release the club properly. My philosophy on this is the same for either release and in fact I said this same thing in the previous chapter in the overview of the LOP release. Some may strongly argue this point and say the body is the lead actor and is not playing a supporting role. I'm not in that camp, especially since this book is about the release, which is overwhelmingly controlled by the actions of the arm and club motor. However that does not in any way diminish the role of the body. Its function is to allow, facilitate and amplify the release. One thing is for certain: if the body motor "fights" what you are trying to accomplish in the release it can TOTALLY DESTROY your efforts. So we need to understand just how your body must react to support your release, not destroy it.

The body motor supports the RIT release in a very different way than it works in the LOP release. In the LOP release the body motor supports a left arm pull, an outward right arm and shaft rotation with a lateral slide and outward thrust of the hips. The body motion in the RIT release is nearly the opposite. The hips and shoulders rotate while the tailbone stays away from any thrust. This motion supports the INWARD CIRCLE CLOSING and circular centripetal force that is used with the RIT release *(FIG. 9-19). Let's look at this body motor motion in closer detail. Notice I've drawn lines as reference points at address on the top of the head and the back of the hips in the down-the-line photos. In the face-on photos I've drawn reference points at the head, hips and spine.

***FIG. 9.19**

The body in the RIT supports the flatter plane inward throwing motion by turning in posture with the right foot down until impact or after. Without the turn in posture you could not create the inward centripetal force and the outward centrifugal motion.

An instant before the start of the downswing, during the transition between the backswing and the downswing, any lateral lower body movement that transfers weight and adds ground forces to the left foot the RIT release golfer needs to make needs to have been completed. It's just fine if it was completed at the end of the backswing before the transition. Just don't shift the hips laterally during the downswing. During the downswing there must be hip rotation not hip slide and then rotation. Once the transition period weight transfer onto the left foot is accomplished, the left hip initiates the downswing body motion and the shoulders quickly join WITH the turning hips.

The big point in this turning motion is what is happening within your turn. There are two big points that must happen. Point one, there must be sufficient backward pressure on your tailbone/pelvis so that when your hips rotate they DO NOT thrust outward. The hips must maintain or even increase their relative distance from the target line. This is crucial because of the radius issue I have previously discussed on two occasions. If the hip position goes outward while turning, the arms and club handle have no room to come downward and inward. A throw would result in the clubhead's coming into impact well beyond the ball. As a result, you will never fully throw/flexion the clubhead. Instead you will drop the shaft vertically because the arms will be too high and too far from you. In essence, you will have turned your RIT release into an LOP release if you hip thrust.

The second point I want to emphasize is the angle your hips and shoulders turn on. As you complete your turn, the entire left side goes up and the right shoulder and right hip go down. However a word of caution on this must be noted. The left side does not go up and the right side does not go down quickly from the start of the downswing. If this happens it is always a sign of a tilting body and not a turning one. I DO NOT WANT you to TILT your body. There should be NO lowering of the right side and rising of the left side independent of a turning motion. As the turn begins, the right side stays up and the left down. I want it to stay that way until after the initial turn of the left hip. Only after the left hip has initiated the downswing and the turning motion of the ENTIRE BODY is under way does the left side start rising and the right side start lowering. Let this rising and lowering be gentle and not abrupt. Any abrupt up or down motion will STOP your turn. I would far rather have the left side go up and the right side go down too late than too early or too abruptly. Correctly executing the turn and gentle up and down motion, accompanied with a correct tailbone position as you turn, ensures you stay in your body posture. It's OK if your spine goes down/increases for the RIT release; just don't allow it to stand up until during the follow through.

One final word of caution on the correct RIT body motion; DO NOT try to gain early or abrupt body speed during the initiation and early stages of the turn. Your arms have not started their inward centripetal force motion where they move downward and inward into the body. With the arms in their extended position at the start of the downswing any effort to gain early body speed will simply thwart your efforts to create inward centripetal force with your arms. Early speed with the body will in fact cause your arms to be thrown outward. Additionally your body will be fighting your extended arm position due to inertia.

With your arms extended out from your body they are in a drag position relative to rotational body speed. It is exactly the same issue you see in figure skaters. They can only turn quickly as their arms come into their body. The closer the arms come into their body the faster they can rotate. This is the same with the RIT body motion. As the arms drop downward and inward and the centripetal force and centrifugal result increases the body gains more and more turning speed. This is the body working in a true swinging motion versus a leverage motion. In the LOP leverage motion the fast and early hip thrust comes to a sudden slowdown/stop which whips the upper body which in turn whips the arms and then the club. Not so with the throwing/swinging RIT motion where everything reaches its maximum speed at impact. In conclusion, allow the body rotation to slowly accelerate to top speed along with the centripetal downward and inward arm drop and the outward centripetal throw.

In review for a correct RIT release body motion:

1) The hips must have completed their lateral motion prior to the start of the downswing.
2) The left hip initiates the downswing turn and shoulders and right hip immediately start turning after this initiating move.
3) As the hips turn, their distance from the target line must be maintained or increased.
4) Along with a correct hip turn, the left side must gently rise and the right shoulder and right hip must gently lower to maintain the spine angle.
5) Allow the body to accelerate gradually in concert with the dropping downward and inward arms.

Correct RIT Release | Playing Draws, Fades and High Shots

The LOP release has the clubface square to the path for only an instant. The clubface is either open or closed to the path for most of the release zone. So playing shots that curve is not difficult. You simply decide which side of a square clubface you want to play on; when it's open and play fades or when it's closed and play draws. With the RIT it's even easier to shape shots. The RIT release hits mostly straight shots because of its very stable clubface to the path. To play draws and fades we need to make only minor adjustments.

To play either shot you merely need to adjust the clubface to your grip; either more closed for a draw or more open for a fade. The photos show you how to do that. Place the club on the ground with an open or closed face and then take your NORMAL grip. Hold the shaft parallel to the ground in front of you to check that the face-to-grip alignment is correct *(FIG. 9.20). Now make the second minor adjustment. Move the ball slightly forward in your stance for a fade and slightly back of normal for a draw. These moves will assure you hit the ball swinging on the correct portion of the in-to-in arc for the shot you're playing *(FIG. 9.21). With the ball back for the draw you'll be hitting the ball while on the outward part of the path/arc so the ball starts just right of the target and curves left onto it. In addition this back in the stance ball placement helps with ensuring the face will be closed to the path (or said differently, the path will be right of the clubface). With the ball forward for the fade you'll hit it on the back to the inside portion allowing for the ball to start slightly left and fade onto the target. It will also help you to have the path left of the clubface (or said differently, the face will be open to the path).

*FIG. 9.20

Photo 1 shows normal grip and normal clubface. Photo 2 shows normal grip and closed clubface. Photo 3 shows normal grip and open clubface.

*FIG. 9.21

Photo 1 shows a closed clubface in normal grip and a ball back in stance. Photo 2 shows an open clubface in normal grip and a ball forward in stance.

You are now ready to make exactly your NORMAL RIT release swing to play the desired shot. There is however one more thing I would suggest you do to ensure you hit the fade or draw shot. While making your NORMAL swing, "SEE" the exact clubface, to ball, to path alignment you set up at address. In the photos I show you the look I want you to be aware of during impact. Too often when playing a draw, the golfer will feel the clubface coming into the ball closed to his path. Since he is used to feeling a square clubface to the path he often will automatically react to the closed face by blocking the throw so the clubface comes into the ball square or sometimes even open.

You don't want the face coming in square to the path and you surely don't want to overreact and have it open; you want it coming in closed to play a draw. But sometimes your brain has an automatic reaction and you make a correction you do not really want to make. It's the same with a fade when your athletic hand-eye coordination senses the clubface is open to the path and wants to roll it closed. To fight this just "see" the clubface to ball and to path alignment that you set up at address, release the club as you always do, and simply remind yourself during the swing to allow the closed or open to the path and to the ball relationship you are trying to achieve to happen.

> In review for the correct RIT release playing draws and fades:
>
> 1) Change the clubface to grip alignment at address.
> 2) Move the ball slightly in your stance; forward to fade, back to draw.
> 3) Make your normal RIT release swing.
> 4) During the swing "see" the desired clubface to path and to ball relationship.

The RIT release generally tends to produce slightly lower shots, especially with the straighter faced clubs off the ground or when hitting shots from longer rough. Hitting high soft shots with a 3 wood or a 3 or 4 iron off of tight lies is sometimes difficult for many RIT release players to execute. Thank goodness we now have hybrids to help gain height on our long irons, but fairway woods off the ground can still be a problem. In addition when faced with shots out of long rough the RIT release player needs the ability to get the ball up quickly. To play higher shots with the RIT release the golfer needs to create a narrower swing that will allow the clubhead to better hit down, under and up during impact *(FIG. 9.22).

Fortunately there's an easy way to do this. It just takes a little practice to get it down. Taking a longer than usual backswing and a longer follow through is all you need to do. By doing this you automatically make the bottom of the swing narrower and will hit higher shots. The only difficult part is getting used to the longer backswing and follow through, because when you first attempt it your timing for the start of your downswing will be off. However it doesn't take many balls or much practice to get used to it. The release zone and impact should purposely feel narrower. You should feel the clubhead come into the ball on a steeper downward angle and come back up after impact on a steeper upward angle. The backswing and downswing are both just a little longer to allow you to make this new bottom of the swing a little narrower.

*FIG. 9.22

For higher shots make a much longer backswing with the clubshaft and a much longer follow through.

> In review of the correct RIT release for higher shots:
>
> 1) Create a narrower bottom to the swing.
> 2) Make a longer backswing and a longer follow through.

In Chapter 9 I included some advice when discussing LOP mistakes. In case you skipped that section I'm going to repeat it now along with some additional material for the RIT mistakes.

Earlier I talked about the two important issues in improving your swing: understanding the correct move and the mistake as well. We've just covered the correct moves, now your next job is to find your mistake, thoroughly understand it and then compare it to the correct moves. By going back and forth between these two parts of this chapter you will gain the necessary insights to correctly execute your release.

Before we look at the various mistakes that can be made while attempting the RIT release, there's something that can help you identify which mistake you may be making, as well as aid in your progress towards a correct release. The use of video is nearly invaluable in accelerating your progress. It will help to identify your mistake as well as chart your progress. Incidentally, I ask every Tour professional I instruct to do the same thing. With the advent of smart phones with great video cameras along with a number of swing analysis apps you can download, you have your very own video studio in your pocket. When you do take a video, take it from down the line at a point halfway between the golfer's feet and the ball; somewhere near what we refer to as the hand line *(FIG. 9.23). Just line up the camera, the hands at address and the target in a straight line. When viewing the video after importing it into an analyzer, you will draw different lines for the RIT release than the line you used for the LOP release. For the RIT release, draw a line up from the heel of the clubhead through the clubshaft and then through the body. The other line will be a parallel line to the shaft plane line across the top of the shoulders. It should look exactly like the address photo for the RIT release. Now everything you compare will be in relation to that shaft plane line for the RIT release.

Fig. 9.23

To analyze the RIT release you need to draw two plane lines at address. One line, the shaft plane line, is drawn from the heel of the club straight up the shaft and through the body. The second line is a parallel line to the shaft plane line drawn across the top of the shoulders.

Incorrect RIT Releases: Arms/Handle Mistakes and Shaft/Clubhead Mistakes

I've divided the mistakes you can typically make into three different categories: mistakes caused by incorrect arm (I also refer to this as incorrect handle) motion, mistakes caused by incorrect shaft (I also refer to this as incorrect clubhead) motion and mistakes caused by both the arms and shaft. Since an RIT release is not only a right arm, inward, throwing motion it also has a plane shift. It requires doing two very separate motions simultaneously: dropping the left arm downward and inward and throwing/flexion of the right wrist. By examining your mistakes relative to which of the two things you are supposed to be doing but in fact are not doing, I believe you can more readily understand the error. Also in giving you the corrections to these mistakes I'll refer to "drills" in the text, as I did for the LOP release. The details of these drills are found in Chapter Ten.

Shaft/Clubhead Mistake: In-To-Out

The predominant ball flight misses for this mistake are hooks, pushes, fat and thin shots. This golfer will struggle both to hit the ball solidly and to hit it accurately. This mistake often comes about when the golfer has the clubface closing faster than the path is arcing to the left. The balls are going left and he needs his path to be less to the right. Unfortunately he is thinking just the opposite. Because his ball is left he thinks he is "over the top" and needs to swing more to the right *(FIG. 9.24). The more he swings to the right the more the clubface keeps closing to the path, hitting the ball to the left. If he

***FIG. 9.24**

The Shaft/Clubhead Mistake in-to-out has the left arm dropping down correctly so the right forearm and handle is on the shaft plane line. Unfortunately the right wrist is not throwing both early enough and far enough and as a result the clubhead is coming down well under the plane line and exiting impact well in front of it.

ever looks at his divot, it's not pointed to the left, it's pointed to the right and the ball is considerably left of the divot's direction. In addition, the divot if any can sometimes occur behind the ball, hitting fat shots, because the in-to-out path tends to bottom-out early. When he isn't taking divots the fat shot turns into a thin shot. Let's see what the release that's causing these ball flight misses looks like.

The key photos for understanding this mistake are at the release zone entry, just past impact and the exit. Let's start with the first one. Notice the arms/handle is on the shaft plane line but the shaft/clubhead is quite far below the line. The arms have swung downward and inward fairly correctly but the shaft/clubhead has dropped/uncocked (ulnar deviation) instead of being thrown outward. Because the shaft is still on the left arm plane, the clubface is still very open. This very open face is also being swung very far in-to out, to the right of the target. Notice the position just after impact—how the clubhead has now moved out in front of the line. This from-behind-and-under-the-line position to above and in front of the line is the evidence of this in-to-out path. Notice in the exit photo, the shaft is not parallel to the line and how much the clubface is rolled over shut. The more upright shaft is an indication of the in-to-out and the shut clubface is showing the left arm plane LOP rollover that occurred to close the face.

To correct this mistake you must begin throwing the shaft/clubhead outward much earlier in the downswing while retarding any uncocking of the left wrist. You must be AWARE of NOT DROPPING the shaft/clubhead, only dropping the arms/handle to get to the ground.

The feel you will have is out-to-in with the shaft/clubhead. Additionally the swing will feel much steeper. Even though your handle is close to the shaft plane line you can also improve your clubshaft position by paying some attention to the action of the arms. With the shaft still aligned with the left arm, the left arm is staying the outside (nearest to the target line) arm. As you throw the shaft outward, shift the left arm hard downward and inward; be conscious the left arm is becoming the inside arm and the right wrist is outside the left arm and the right arm is becoming the outside plane arm. This will make your work to get the clubshaft thrown outward a lot easier.

As much as both these moves might feel like an out-to-in swing, I assure you, you will not swing out-to-in, as long as you continue to drop your left arm/handle downward and inward. Again you must "find the ground" with the arms/handle drop—not with the shaft/clubhead dropping. The photos showing the "Throw and Drop" drill from Chapter Ten illustrates what you will need to feel. It's a motion that stops short of impact with the arms/handle low and tight to you and the shaft/clubhead thrown outward. This is an exaggeration of what you will actually do but I want you to feel exactly like the drill looks. When you've improved the first part of the release with a throw of the shaft instead of a dropping motion, the photos in the mistake just after impact and exit should also improve. If hooking is still a problem after working on and improving the early part of the release, taking a look at the exit position in a video of your swing will undoubtedly show there is some rollover still going on. To rid yourself of the rollover, the photo of Ben Hogan in the "Three Finger Throw" drill shown in Chapter Ten will help. Read the entire drill in Chapter Ten and continue to work on it until you do it the right way.

Arms/Handle and Shaft/Clubhead Mistake: In-To-Out

This like the previous mistake is a directional mistake: It's too much in-to-out. The difference however is this mistake is made with both the forearm/handle and the shaft/clubhead being out of position *(FIG. 9.25). In other words, both ends of the club are wrong for the RIT release. Because the shaft is far too vertical for the shaft plane line, the ROC for you is very high. It's that very high clubface rate of closure that causes ball flight misses that go wildly both right and left. Your clubface is unstable to the path/plane throughout the release zone. In fact it's so unstable even trying to play draws and fades as in the LOP release is not reliable because the shaft is so upright to the flatter swing forces. This upright shaft to flatter swing forces will result in the clubface coming into the release zone even more open and closing even more rapidly than in the LOP. This is army golf—left, right, left, right.

This particular mistake is a little harder to fix because both ends of the club are off plane. Your right forearm/handle motion is wrong because you are pulling downward and outward with the left arm as the plane arm. You are trying to line up the plane to hit the ball with your left arm pointed at the target line. Remember, in the RIT release, you are not on plane to hit the ball at the top of your backswing. You have two choices, a correct one and a wrong one, to get on a plane that will hit the ball. For an RIT release you've chosen the wrong way. You are actually using the LOP release, swinging the club at the ball using your left arm as the plane arm. That's why your handle is so high above the shaft plane line and why you have to drop the shaft/clubhead just to hit the ball.

***FIG. 9.25**

In this in-to-out mistake both ends of the club are wrong. The handle is too far above the shaft plane line due to the left arm not dropping down and in. The clubhead has been unhinged/uncocked below the line instead of being thrown outward.

I want you to choose the other way to hit the ball by forming a plane to hit the ball through a plane shift down onto the shaft plane with the right arm as the plane arm. You need to line up the clubshaft with the right forearm, get the left arm down and inward vertically so it is totally out of the way, and hit with the right wrist and arm. Remember, to form that new plane directed at the ball you need two equal elements: an outward/horizontal element and a vertical/downward/inward element. You also need to do them together. The outward/horizontal element is the right wrist throw/flexion while the vertical/downward/inward part is the left arm/handle drop. You are currently doing the reverse with horizontal outward arms and a vertical dropping clubhead.

The drill you need to help you accomplish this is the "Throw and Drop" drill discussed in the previous in-to-out mistake and fully detailed in Chapter Ten. I can't overstate how much you need to feel the outward shaft throw and the downward/inward to vertical left arm drop being done simultaneously. Right now you are doing neither and the usual thing people want to do is deal with two issues one at a time. Trust me, this will not work. Even though both the arm drop and the shaft throw are things you've never done you have to learn to do them at the same time. So what I'm going to do is work our way into doing it. With the "Throw and Drop" drill keep flexing your right wrist so the shaft/clubhead goes outward, and drop your left arm/handle downward/inward to a spot just short of impact. Feel if you did it wrong by dropping the shaft/clubhead or if you did it correctly by throwing the shaft/clubhead outward. Next try to feel that you drop your left arm downward and inward with NO PULLING outward of the left arm. It was the pulling of the left arm at the ball/target line that got you into this mess. So instead, feel your left arm is NOT SWINGING AT THE BALL as it drops to vertical while you throw the right wrist.

Keep doing this drill over and over, checking that you've performed each element correctly. Now you're ready to take the drill to the next step. We are going to do the drill in a quick series three times. Bring the drill down to just short of impact two times but on the third time swing right on through impact to a swing finish by simply continuing to swing your right forearm/handle around your torso and throw the right wrist. Feel the low and inward forearm/handle move very close to you while the throw takes you around to the finish. Your finish should "feel" much lower and a lot farther around you to the left. *(FIG. 9.26). Improvement should be fairly immediate. With your naturally rounded backswing and then an off-plane-to-your-swing-forces upright shaft you were caught with a release that has the highest ROC you could possibly have. The clubface was very unstable and only for the briefest moment was it square to the path you were swinging on. It was wide open one instant and then very closed the next. As you improve, even if you are not yet where you ultimately want to be (on the shaft plane line) you will get a more and more stable clubface and the shots will be less wild and more often in play At some point in your improvement I also want you to improve your exit using the "Three Finger Throw" drill discussed in the previous mistake lesson and detailed in Chapter Ten.

One final note on this mistake's correction, the body can oftentimes be thrusting outward and the arms/handle cannot come into you close enough to correct the in-to-out swing *(FIG. 9.27). If this is showing up in your analysis, then at some point after you have worked on throwing early and on the impact throw as well, you may need to get your hips to turn better. I show the "Anti-Hip Thrust" drill in

*Fig. 9.26

You will feel a much lower and flatter follow through.

*FIG. 9.27

An outward hip thrust shoves the pelvis towards the ball and forces the spine to dramatically rise.

Chapter Ten and you may need to work on it. The reason I'm not giving it to you now is your mistake usually doesn't have a bad hip thrusting problem. There's another one coming up similar to yours that does. Any hip thrust you may have should go away naturally, athletically, by throwing the clubshaft outward earlier in the downswing and as a result of the throw, moving your left arm/handle differently. I believe in this case the body motor is a support motor and, in a short time, will change its movements almost automatically to support the new wrist flexion and arm motion.

*FIG. 9.28

This out-to-in mistake originates with the arms being thrown outward along with the clubshaft.

Shaft/Clubhead Mistake: Out-To-In

The ball flight misses a golfer hits with this mistake are slices, pulls, sky balls with the driver, and possibly a low trap ball with fairway woods and long irons. This mistake creates a steep impact and is usually accompanied by bouts of deep divot taking, particularly with short and middle irons. Sometimes this golfer overreacts to the steep angles right at impact and swings upward so fiercely that he will take no divot at all.

Take note of the photos illustrating this mistake. Note the shaft/clubhead is thrown outward but the arms/handle also is thrown outward. This is not a terribly difficult mistake to fix because the entire golf club is close to parallel to the shaft plane, just a bit beyond it *(FIG. 9.28). You obviously need to drop the left arm/handle downward and inward to vertical while keeping the right elbow back along the seam of your shirt, right from the top, while still throwing the shaft outward. Your outward throw was not done with the right wrist. You threw the shaft outward along with the entire arm. I don't want you to throw the arm out; just the shaft, using just the wrist while you drop the left arm/handle. You are the exact opposite to the golfer in the first mistake above—the Shaft/Clubhead In-To-Out Mistake golfer. You might want to read his lesson because it's the opposite of yours. Your clubhead is fine; your left arm/handle is what's wrong. The drills in Chapter Ten that will help you the most are the "Knife in the Groin" drill, "Under Arm Throw" drill and the "Three Finger Throw" drill.

The "Knife in the Groin" is one of Peter Jacobsen's favorites. It helps you drop the left arm downward and inward towards your groin so it gets out of the way and becomes the inward/non-plane arm. In the "Under Arm Throw" drill photo you can see how the right arm drops straight down by the right leg as though you were pitching a softball out towards the golf ball. When executing this drill feel the right arm very low, close and tight to your right side, but please remember to still throw the shaft outward with your right wrist while it's busy bowling. In using the "Three Finger Throw" drill discussed in several of these mistake lessons and detailed in Chapter Ten, learning how to continue flexing the right wrist all the way through the impact zone without any clubhead or right forearm roll-over.

Arms/Handle Mistake: Clubhead on Plane, Handle Above

There's good news and bad news for this mistake. The good news is the clubhead is on plane; the golfer will hit very good shots. He will hit the ball solidly, but suffer directionally. The bad news is the handle is too high, above the plane line, and as a result the shaft is a little too upright *(FIG. 9.29). Although the shaft is not as upright as for someone on the shoulder plane line, it still creates some ROC problems. As noted earlier in this book, the longer the shaft is held on the left arm plane, two things occur: The face is held open a long time and the higher and farther from us the handle is located. The high/far handle creates an upright shaft; the higher/farther it is the more upright the shaft.

*FIG. 9.29

With the handle too high above the shaft plane line there is too high a ROC to hit repetitive ball flights for the RIT release.

The combination of upright shaft and open clubface creates a high ROC. The higher the ROC the more the clubface is unstable to the path. Since this RIT mistake creates a plane more upright than the shaft plane line but well below a shoulder plane line, the ROC with this release is less than with the LOP release on the shoulder plane line but greater than with the RIT on the shaft plane line. In essence the problem with having the clubhead on plane but the handle above is the golfer will hit great shots but have just enough unstable clubface to hit some untimely wild shots. This golfer is capable of winning and playing great golf and also capable of seemingly losing it all overnight. This golfer is actually the RIT hybrid I spoke of in an earlier chapter. He needs to go in one of two ways.

He needs to stay with the LOP release but incorporate either a stronger grip at address or a bowed left wrist (closed position) at the top of his backswing, or both. By doing so, he can now swing down into impact on the left arm plane without the clubface being so unmanageably open. He can cut down on the ROC that is giving him so much difficulty in being consistent. The tradeoff is sometimes a loss of distance or a loss of ball flight height. Reread that area in Chapter Seven about the RIT hybrid before you make the decision. Do you want to become a hybrid or do you want to correct your RIT release?

To correct this RIT mistake the golfer needs to get the left arm/handle lower, and his left arm has to quit blocking both the full release of the right wrist and the right forearm from becoming the plane arm. The left arm is not only not dropping downward and inward enough; it is also checking the clubhead from getting whipped around to the left on plane with the completion of the right wrist throw/flexion. There are two drills that will help correct this mistake. Those are the "Knife in the Groin" drill and the "Three Finger Throw" drill. Both drills are detailed in the next chapter. The "Knife in the Groin" drill is a highly visual drill and effective at getting the left arm/handle to come downward and inward. As you've probably figured out by now if you've been reading all the RIT mistakes, the "Three Finger Throw" is a favorite of mine and will help with the blocking of the wrist throw.

CHAPTER TEN

SWING PHOTOS & DRILLS

COMPARISIONS | TIGER WOODS
Driver vs. Iron

COMPARISIONS | DAVID DUVAL
1997 vs. 2012

COMPARISIONS | MATT KUCHAR
Under Plane Truth instruction, Matt Kuchar went from #301 in the OWGR to #4.

COMPARISIONS | SCOTT PIERCY

Under Plane Truth instruction, Scott Piercy went from #435 in the OWGR to #36.

LOP | PHIL MICKELSON

LOP | LUKE DONALD

LOP | BERNHARD LANGER

LOP | ANNIKA SORENSTAM

LOP | KARRIE WEBB

LOP | CRISTIE KERR

LOP HYBRID | ZACH JOHNSON

RIT | HENRIK STENSON

RIT | ADAM SCOTT

RIT | LEE WESTWOOD

RIT | SUZANN PETTERSEN

RIT | SE RI PAK

RIT HYBRID | JIM FURYK

RIT HYBRID | JOHN DALY

LOP DRILLS | RIGHT HAND PRESSURE

The purpose of this drill is to slow down the high ROC for the LOP. It is particularly helpful for golfers who are hooking too much. The key to this drill is locating two pressure points. One point is at the base of your right palm, right at the end of your lifeline, just below the thumb. The photo shows exactly where this spot is *(DLOP-1). To locate the second pressure point take your grip. Now with your grip in place, the right palm pressure point you've located is going to touch the top part of your left thumb *(DLOP-2). The second pressure point is exactly where it touches the top of the thumb. It is these two pressure points, one at the base of you right palm and the other on top of your left thumb that I want welded together during the release zone. The motion of the right forearm during the release zone for an LOP release is an outward counterclockwise movement. During this outward rolling right forearm move, feel as though there is something soft between the two pressure points and squeeze the soft object HARD so the two points become welded together. Your right hand will have rolled on top of the left hand while this pressure is being applied. I want your right hand on top of the left. I just don't want the hands to come apart and separate while this is happening. If they come apart and slap while also rotating the ROC becomes so uncontrollable you can't predict much of anything except an out of play hook. By squeezing the pressure points together you eliminate any unwanted loose slapping motion of the wrists while rotating the right forearm. In fact, the harder you squeeze the less you will draw the ball and you may even start to hit a fade.

*DLOP-1

The pressure point on the right hand is on the lifeline at the base of the thumb.

*DLOP-2

The pressure point on the left thumb is exactly where the right hand pressure point touches the left thumb. With the grip in place squeeze these two points together.

LOP DRILLS | BOWLING

This drill is very similar with only minor differences to the under arm throw for the RIT release. Both are designed to help the golfer who is struggling with an out to in release pattern. The players who have this problem are usually hitting slices, pulls, chops, chunks and sky balls as their ball flight misses. This drill is an excellent one to use in conjunction with the "Lateral Hip Slide" and the "Hip Thrust" drills.

To execute this drill I want you to make an underarm bowling motion while standing at address to a golf ball. Begin your arm swing about shoulder high BEHIND you. Now as your downward/underarm motion reaches its lowest point just behind your right hip and starts to rise upward and outward, I want you to slightly roll your right forearm counterclockwise and bowl a hooking ball out towards the ball at address *(DLOP-3). Do this several times until the underarm bowling motion is natural. Now grip a club in both hands, go to address and then take your normal backswing. Stop at the top of your backswing and remove your left hand. From here, concentrate on swinging your right arm in an underarm bowling motion. At about the lowest point which should be very near your right leg, start bowling the clubhead outward with some right forearm counterclockwise rotation and time it so the bowling throw will be completed when your underarm motion swings up and out towards the ball *(DLOP-4).

*DLOP-3

Swing the right arm and rotate it counterclockwise from the right side outward towards the ball in an underhand bowling motion as though bowling a hook ball.

*DLOP-4

With a club in your right hand, bowl the club outward from your right side towards the ball while rotating your right arm.

Once you successfully executed the bowling drill one handed several times put both hands on the club and execute the drill. The feel should be as though you are swinging through the downswing and the release zone decidedly to the right of the target. That's referred to as in to out and is the opposite of what you had been doing.

LOP DRILLS | LATERAL HIP SLIDE

This drill is designed to help the golfer who swings out to in and spins/backs up his hips during the downswing. A lateral hip slide is a very important move for the LOP release during the initial stages of the downswing. The lateral move ensures the lower body will be closer to the target than the upper body during the first half of the downswing and helps create space for the arms to drop downward from the top of backswing. The golfer in need of this drill has been turning his hips too fast and too soon right at the start of the downswing and is leaving too much weight on his right foot *(DLOP-5). As a result of this faulty hip move the arms swing down to much out to in. This drill is excellent to use in conjunction with the "Hip Thrust" and "Bowling" drills.

To execute this drill, place an empty water bottle or a Styrofoam noodle on a stick. Position it while at address as in the photo just barely outside the tip of the left shoe with the water bottle or noodle positioned hip high, a few inches target side of the hip and just slightly in front of the hip. Grip a club and swing to the top of your backswing. From here, in a practice swing with no ball, bump your hips laterally towards the target until you hit the object on the stick. I want you to

*DLOP-5

This mistake has the golfer twisting his hips away from the target instead of towards it.

*DLOP-6

Start the downswing by laterally moving your hips so the left hip contacts the water bottle. Then turn the hips keeping them against the bottle.

feel this move transfers weight to your left foot. Do this a number of times WITHOUT swinging the club down *(DLOP-6). Now repeat as before but just after bumping the stick object, transfer some weight to your left foot and drop your arms VERTICALLY to a spot just short of impact. Keep bumping the object and dropping your arms vertically. After success with this, go ahead and swing your arms through to the finish after the bump, weight shift and vertical drop. Once you get the feel for how the lateral hip slide drill works, start hitting balls with slow deliberate actions that mimic the drill. As you feel more and more comfortable, work up to normal speed.

LOP DRILLS | HIP THRUST

This is the last of three LOP drills I recommend in conjunction with each other; the "Bowling" drill, the "Lateral Hip Slide" and this one, the "Hip Thrust" drill. All three drills are specifically for the out to in LOP golfer whose ball flight misses are slices, pulls, chops, chunks and sky balls. I leave this drill for last because it can become dangerous so I need to forewarn you of the health problems if you hip thrust too hard or too much. A big or hard hip thrust can result in hyperextending your lower back during the follow through. This is the common "golfer's bad back" and although you will see in the LOP photos of great golfers that most all of them hip thrust and raise their spines during impact, do so with caution. Some hip thrust is a wonderful thing for the LOP golfer, a lot of it can be harmful.

To execute this drill, address a ball, make a practice backswing and stop. Now in measured movements, slide your hips laterally and at one and the same time thrust your right hip and thigh forward and outward towards a spot just in front of the ball. Do not yet swing your arms down. Keep repeating this initial downswing move and be conscious that your head stays fairly still while making the lateral hip move and thrust *(DLOP-7, also see DRIT-18,19 & 20). Once you have successfully repeated this, do it again but allow the arms to swing down after the slide and thrust. I want you to be particular about feeling two things; 1) the arms are dropping down on the inside near your right leg and 2) the clubface is slightly opening. A correct hip thrust will accomplish both these things. You want the clubface slightly rotating clockwise open in the first half of the downswing. That will set it up to rotate counterclockwise closing during the release zone. Now make practice swings in normal tempo all the way through the release zone to the finish. Keep trying to feel the slide and thrust

*DLOP-7

Initiate the downswing with a lateral left hip move and an outward right hip thrust. The arms will drop down close to your right leg with the clubface slightly open.

INITIATES the downswing and that it PRECEEDS the arm swing. Also feel when the arms do swing they drop down close to your right leg and then out towards the ball. When you are confident you have executed the drill correctly, then start hitting shots. The ball flight will tell you if and when you are making progress.

LOP DRILLS | TARGET LINE STICK

This drill is designed for the golfer whose ball flight misses are hooks, pushes, fat and thin shots. One of the primary causes for these shots is an in to out swing path. If he takes a divot it will always be to the right of the target. Any ball left of his target will also be far left of his divot direction. One of the main objectives of the LOP is to be able to hit quality predictable shots on either side of a square clubface. That would mean hitting controllable fades and draws. Uncontrollable fades and draws are slices and hooks. This happens when the swing path starts moving too far in to out or too far out to in. As long as the swing path is consistently in to in, playing solid, high quality draws and fades is pretty simple and predictable. It when that path strays too far from in to in that the shots lose their quality and predictability.

This drill is an excellent way to correct the too far in to out swing path and make it a more neutral in to in path. To execute the drill you will need an alignment stick and place it on your target line approximately 10 to 12 feet in front of the ball *(DLOP-8). The objective is to hit a shot that starts left of the stick and fades to the right. To do this I want the golfer to aim parallel to the target line with the

*DLOP-8

Place an alignment stick on the target line approximately 10-12 ft. in front of the ball.

*DLOP-9

With the ball forward in the stance, swing the arms and club more out-to-in across the ball left until the ball starts left of the stick and fades to the right.

ball played approximately 3 or 4 inches farther forward in their stance than normal. This will make it easier to get their swing path more to the left *(DLOP-9). What I want is a path far enough left with a face slightly open to that path so the ball starts left of the stick and fades back. Keep swinging left until the ball starts left of the stick and fades. If the ball is starting left but is not fading or is going even farther left, the swing path is still not left of the clubface. Start slowing down the closing face and increase the leftward path until you get it correct; a ball that starts left of the stick and fades.

AIT DRILLS | THREE FINGER THROW

This drill is designed to help you with the correct flexion of the right wrist throughout the release zone. Additionally it aids in correcting any rollover of the clubhead and right forearm during the throw. To execute this drill grip a club as shown *(DRIT-1) with only your right hand using just the last three fingers keeping your thumb and

***DRIT-1**

Hold the club in only the last three fingers of your right hand keeping the thumb and index finger off the club.

index finger totally off the club. Using only the last three fingers helps you throw the club more horizontally around because the only fingers on the club are UNDER the shaft. The thumb and index finger ride ON TOP of the shaft and can often create excessive vertical force causing the clubhead to drop under the shaft line. They additionally can cause rollover force on the club. Both of these forces we are trying to avoid in the RIT release. Next approximate a starting spot just above waist high in your downswing. You are going to throw the clubhead past the handle using a half side-on, half underarm motion. Where you throw the club is very important. In looking at the photos which show the entire throwing motion, you can note the clubhead is being thrown up the plane and behind you on an approximate 45 degree angle *(DRIT-2). The exact location your right hand is throwing towards is mid-ribcage under your left arm with the inside of your forearm pointing half upward and half behind you. This is also the direction I want the clubhead thrown in; which

*DRIT-2

Throw the clubhead past the handle in a half-sidearm/half-underarm motion with NO ROLLOVER of the forearm.

is up the plane. Throw the club several times until you can feel the arm and wrist throwing and you get the club thrown in the correct plane. If when you have tried throwing and you are hooking or rolling over the clubhead, then when you throw the club in this drill you will want to have the inside of your right forearm pointed slightly to the sky with your palm looking straight back at you and your fingers pointing more upward. In doing this you will feel slight clockwise pressure on your right forearm while throwing the right wrist. Just make sure in an effort to throw with your right forearm more inside facing up, that your wrist achieves a fully flexed position. Throwing with this clockwise pressure on your right forearm holding your thumb and index finger off the club will help you eliminate any vertical dropping or rolling over of the clubhead.

Next I want you to make the same half swing throwing motion using both hands on the club but still using the same right hand grip with the thumb and index finger off the club. After several swings try hitting balls with this grip and half swing. If the first few shots are not very good, just keep trying until you are finding the ball. The club is being thrown around more horizontally and you might not be correctly dropping your left arm downward and inward (see THROW AND DROP drill). Finally, as lightly as possible, place the thumb and forefinger on the club and again hit balls using the same half swing throwing motion with all right hand grip pressure

*DRIT-3

Note the exaction position of Ben Hogan's wrists and hands. The right wrist is in full flexion and the left wrist is in full extension. The forearms have not turned over and the back of his right hand is facing the target.

concentrated in the last three fingers. I want you to come to a finish exactly like the photo of Ben Hogan *(DRIT-3). Check yourself at the end of each drill swing to see if your wrists are just like his. The left wrist should be in extension and the right wrist in flexion. Now hit some full swing shots. If again you are hooking or rolling over the clubhead make sure your grip pressure is correct.

RIT DRILLS | KNIFE IN THE GROIN

This drill illustrates an exaggeration of the exact location towards where the left arm drops downward and inward. The idea is to imagine a knife sticking upward out of the end of the club's grip and to forcefully stab it into your left inner thigh. This spot is just inside of where the top of the grip is located at address *(DRIT-4). The location at address is approximately where you want to return the left arm/handle and is the center of your throwing motion. The "Knife in the Groin" is visual drill that not only exaggerates the address position I want your left arm and club handle to return to in the release zone but also illustrates the force you need to accomplish this. Your swing is trying to throw the left arm out away from you like it does in an LOP release. To counter that outward force you must make a decided effort to "stab" the left arm/handle downward and inward so the radius is correct for the throwing motion.

*DRIT-4

Pretend there is a knife pointing straight out of the grip end of the golf club. While throwing the clubhead outward and around with the right wrist, stick the knife into the groin area of the left leg with your left arm.

RIT DRILLS | THROW & DROP

The release requires a somewhat parallel plane drop from the top of backswing down onto the shaft plane line established at address *(DRIT-5). This is essential for success in the release. The two parallel plane lines representing the top of backswing and the shaft plane at address are not exactly 45 degrees to the ground but they are close enough for us to say the shift from the top line to the bottom one requires fairly equal measures of downward/vertical forces and outward/horizontal forces. To illustrate that, a graph line of 45 degrees would be plotted by always finding points that are equally vertical and horizontal. When those points are connected the result is a 45 degree line. It's the same with this drill. When you try to execute a horizontal throw of the clubhead and at the same time drop your left arm down into a vertical position the result will be a shaft that drops onto the shaft plane line. It will be a huge help for you when executing this drill if you have the availability of video or a mirror. You will want to locate them to your right at address in a down the target line position so you can watch your efforts to make a correct plane shift. The idea is to coordinate the throwing motion of the clubhead from behind your right arm to in front of it while at the same time dropping your left arm vertically. To easily move into this drill I will want you to go to the

DRIT-5

The RIT release requires a parallel drop from the top of backswing plane onto to the address shaft plane.

top of your backswing. From there you will do this drill in three very different ways. First I want you to simply throw the clubhead out from behind your right arm while leaving your left arm approximately where it was at the top. Your left arm might lower just a bit to accommodate a complete throw but make it look as close to the photo as you can *(DRIT-6). After doing several of these now I want you to do the opposite. From the top of backswing do not throw the clubhead but instead lower your left arm vertically downward as much as you can. Again you may have some outward movement of the clubhead but try to match the photo as close as you can *(DRIT-7). After several successful attempts at this lets do the two motions together.

Go to the top of your backswing and try coordinating the outward throw of the clubhead from behind the right arm and dropping the left arm to a vertical position. Keep doing it until you can match the photos *(DRIT-8). Now notice a few things. First, at the end of the throw and drop the clubhead isn't quite on the ground. Right now I don't want it to be. I'll get to that in a moment. Just try and match the photos. If when you watch yourself doing this drill in the mirror the clubhead is coming out faster than the handle is dropping (see photo) *(DRIT-9) then slow down the outward throw until the downward drop and throw match up. Conversely if the clubhead is lagging behind the vertical drop (see photo) *(DRIT-10) then slow down the drop and get the throw going outward better until they match up. This coordination is very important to understand because when you start hitting balls if you don't do it correctly you'll want to know what exactly you are doing wrong. The answer will be either you aren't throwing enough and/or you aren't dropping enough.

*DRIT-6

These photos illustrate a right wrist throw without the arms moving.

*DRIT-7

These photos illustrate a left arm downward and inward drop without any throw.

*DRIT-8

Shows a correct coordination of throwing and dropping the left arm at the same time.

*DRIT-9

Shows an incorrect coordination where the right wrist throwing motion has happened more rapidly than the left arm dropping motion.

*DRIT-10

Shows an incorrect coordination where the left arm is dropping but the right wrist isn't sufficiently throwing the clubhead outward and around.

*DRIT-11

These photos illustrate the correct coordination of throw and drop and allowing the clubhead to return to the ground.

Or you just aren't coordinating the efforts. After several successful tries let's try doing it so the clubhead comes all the way down *(DRIT-11). Please keep rehearsing the drill by first throwing the clubhead out from behind the right arm, then just lowering the left arm to vertical, and finally coordinating them. After a while you'll get the hang of it and you're ready to start hitting some balls.

Hitting balls is when video really comes in handy. With some software apps you can draw in a shaft plane line and check yourself when hitting a ball in exactly the same way you did in the mirror. And remember if it isn't correct there are only three answers; 1) either you are not throwing enough *(DRIT-12) or dropping enough *(DRIT-13), 2) you are not doing both the throw and drop enough *(DRIT-14), or 3) you are not coordinating the effort. If you are hitting the ground behind the ball, you are dropping the clubhead instead of throwing it outward. If you are topping the ball you are not lowering the left arm downward and inward. If you are hooking the ball you are rolling the clubface over after you throw it outward instead of continuing the right wrist flexion/throw through impact with no roll over.

*DRIT-12

This position shows a good left arm drop but insufficient outward clubhead throw.

*DRIT-13

This position shows a correct throw but insufficient left arm downward and inward drop.

*DRIT-14

This position shows neither enough left arm drop or right hand throw. In fact this is a classic LOP position where the left arm has pulled outward and downward while uncocking the left wrist.

RIT DRILLS | UNDERARM THROW

This drill is an excellent cure for golfers who while throwing the clubhead outward cannot drop their left arm to a vertical position right from the top of backswing. Instead the left arm is thrown outward along with the clubhead. This swing mistake usually results in an out to in swing path. The ball flight errors are slices, pulls, chops, chunks and sky balls. The underarm throw teaches you how to still throw the right wrist but at the same time get the arms to drop. To execute this drill hold a golf ball in the fingers of your right hand *(DRIT-1). I want you to make an underarm softball throw while standing at address to a golf ball. Begin your arm swing about shoulder high BEHIND you. Now as your underarm motion reaches its lowest point I want you to throw the golf ball in your hand, just like a softball pitcher, out towards the ball at address *(DRIT-15). Do this several times until the underarm throw is natural. Now with a club in only your right hand, go to address and then approximate a one armed backswing. From the top of your backswing, concentrate on swinging your right arm in an underarm motion. At about half way down, start throwing the clubhead outward and time it so the throw will be completed when your underarm swing reaches its lowest point *(DRIT-16).

Once you successfully executed the underarm throw drill one handed several times put both hands on the club and execute the drill. The feel should be as though you are swinging through the downswing and the release zone decidedly to the right of the target. That's referred to as in to out and is the opposite of what you had been doing.

*DRIT-15

Hold a golf ball in the fingers of the right hand and make an underhand motion to toss the ball out towards an imaginary ball on the target line.

*DRIT-16

While holding a club in only the right hand toss the clubhead in an underhand motion outward in an effort to hit the ball one handed.

RIT DRILLS | ANTI-HIP THRUST

This drill is two drills in one. The first part is to understand and feel what's causing the hip thrust and the second part gives you an exaggerated feel for your correction. The hip thrust is a supporting body motion for an LOP release. It supports a powerful outward release of the right arm and club usually on an in to out path. At the start of the downswing a hip thrust's initial motion is a lateral slide which allows the arms and club to drop down on the inside. This lateral slide is quickly followed by the right hip and right thigh moving upward, forward and outward towards a spot just in front of the ball *(DRIT-17). The right foot also comes up onto the toe very early. As a result of the lateral hip move and thrust there is a spine tilt formed away from the target that holds the upper body behind the lower body. As the thrust reaches its limits the spine raises vertically *(DRIT-18). Unfortunately for the golfer with a hip thrust, when the hips rotate to face the target it often times creates a "reverse C". Reverse C's are a cause of bad backs *(DRIT-19). They are a result of the spine tilt set up in the initial stages of the lateral hip slide and thrust so when the golfer turns his hips to the target he often hyperextends his lower back.

To eliminate the hip thrust the first thing the golfer needs to do is correct the arm swing pattern. An RIT release is an inward not outward release. The inward arm action is not compatible with an outward hip thrust. If the golfer stubbornly keeps working on his RIT release hopefully his athletic instincts will change his body motor pattern. The inward movement of the RIT is aimed at the left thigh

*DRIT-17

These photos illustrate a hip thrust. Note the right hip has thrusted outward and the clubshaft dropped downward too much to the inside.

*DRIT-18

As the hip thrust reaches impact the spine angle has vertically moved upward.

*DRIT-19

Too often a golfer with a hip thrust will finish the swing in a back injury causing reverse "C" position.

(see "Knife in the Groin" drill) and this inward motion alone should be nearly enough to get the left hip moving in a correct manner. The thrust has the left hip sliding and the right hip moving outward. The correct hip movement for a RIT release has the left hip turning leftward of the target, turning behind you, while the right hip is moving in a more lateral motion towards the target. Ever hear, "turn the left hip out of the way"? Well this is it. You turn the left hip back behind you, out of the way, so the right hip, and in fact, the entire right side can come forward towards the target. A good drill for this is to stand at address with your hips just slightly away from a wall or against a railing. At the top of your backswing I want your right hip to have turned back so it is now slightly touching the wall/rail *(DRIT-20). During the transition and as you begin the downswing with a slight shift of the weight to the left foot and start turning the left hip back towards the wall, hold the right hip against the wall/rail and ever so slightly move it laterally along the wall until the left hip has returned to the wall/rail. Once the left hip has reached the wall/rail, the right hip can now move slightly outward and mostly forward as the left hip continues to turn into the wall/rail. The key to this drill is keeping the right hip back until the left hip has had its chance to turn back to the wall/rail. The hip thruster wants to immediately fire his right hip and thigh outward during the initial stages of the downswing. You have to learn to hold it back for a moment and fire the other hip, the left one, backwards behind you. If you employ this new hip movement, you will find it easy to keep your spine bent outward and stay in your posture. In fact as you move your hips correctly and execute your RIT "inward" release you may even feel the desire to lower your spine slightly in the downswing to accommodate the RIT release. Many great RIT golfers do this.

*DRIT-20

At address set up about a fist away from the railing. In the backswing put the right hip against the railing. During the transition and first part of the downswing continue to keep the right hip back against the rail and slide it a few inches towards the target and at the same time bring the left hip back to it so both hips for a moment in time are against the rail. As the hips continue to turn into and through impact the right hip will come off the railing BUT KEEP THE LEFT HIP AGAINST IT AS LONG AS YOU CAN.